The Dysfunctional Church

by
William T Jones, Jr.

Vincom, Inc.
Tulsa, Oklahoma

Unless otherwise indicated, al Scripture quotations are taken from the *King James Version* of the Bible.

The Dysfunctional Church
ISBN 0-927936-44-5
Copyright © 1994 by
William T. Jones, Jr.
316 Sturbridge Village
Hazelwood, MO 63048

Published by Vincom, Inc.
P. O. Box 702400
Tulsa, OK 74170
(918) 254-1276

Dedication

This book is dedicated to my anointed and loving wife, Willie Izetta Jones. Your companionship has taught me to be a functional man of God.

It is also dedicated to my church family, The Greater Mt. Zion Christian Fellowship, and to the Holy Spirit, Who is the source of my inspiration.

God bless you church family, I am proud to be called your pastor. Stay sweet and functional.

— *William T. Jones, Jr.*

In Appreciation

Thank God for you, Bishop T. D. Jakes, for the rich deposits you have placed in my life and for being available in times of tremendous hurt. It is a blessing to know that men can be men and still cry on one's shoulder.

- *William T. Jones, Jr.*

Contents

Contents

Introduction

"I beseech you therefore, brethren, by the mercies of
God, that ye present your bodies a living sacrifice, holy,
acceptable unto God, which is your reasonable service.
And be not conformed to this world: but be ye
transformed by the renewing of your mind, that ye may
prove what is that good, and acceptable, and perfect, will
of God."

Romans 12:1,2

The words of the apostle Paul to those called to be
saints in the province of Rome, are powerful words of
admonition that are very much applicable to all believers!
Many Christians today who are endeavoring to live
"separated" lives have been bombarded by unrighteousness in their communities and feel the pull to conform.

Family structures have broken down to an all-time
statistical low; physical, mental and emotional abuse is
rampant; morals and value systems are grossly forsaken;
chemical-dependent drug abuse is destroying countless
lives daily; personal, corporate and public crime has
undoubtedly doubled in many regions; and people all
over the world are hurting on deep levels! They have
trusted in governmental officials, family, friends, jobs, local
church leaders, tele-evangelists, and all have failed them
miserably. Rebellion, manipulation, and deception have
been around since the Garden of Eden, and still today, we
witness their effects as unrighteous people use them for
power, political and personal gain.

The people of God, as well as sinners today, are searching for practical, down-to-earth instruction in righteousness straight from the Word of God, undiluted, inspired by the Holy Spirit, spoken by a holy, upright preacher or teacher. Pastor William T. Jones, Jr. has felt the pain and sorrow of hurting people all over the world who are tired of being used, abused and rejected; tired of compromising leaders and tired of following traditions of men which yield no real substance or value to their spiritual lives.

The subtle work of the enemy (Satan), needs to be exposed, and the eyes of God's people should be opened so that *light* and *truth* can penetrate their lives and the Holy Spirit will empower them to live holy and righteous in an unholy and unrighteous environment.

The Dysfunctional Church is a book that will speak to many believers and those seeking to know God, who are caught in the trap of tradition and deception, but are praying fervently for liberty and freedom in Christ. It exposes the deceit of false teachers, preachers and prophets, and is "MUST" reading for all audiences, laymen, church pastors and leaders, political and public leaders, and all who are searching for truth. The language used is easy to read and understand. It is written to uncover the trickery of fancy-talking deceivers.

The Dysfunctional Church

1
The Tragedy of Being in the Wrong Church

And he was teaching in one of the synagogues on the sabbath.

And, behold, there was a woman which had a spirit of infirmity eighteen years, and was bowed together, and could in no wise lift up herself.

And when Jesus saw her, he called her to him, and said unto her, Woman, thou art loosed from thine infirmity.

And he laid his hands on her: and immediately she was made straight, and glorified God.

Luke 13:10-13

The Gospel of Luke is the only one of the Gospels that includes the story of this woman afflicted by a spirit of infirmity. Luke was a physician, so he particularly noticed things related to healing and deliverance concerning bodily infirmities in the ministry of Jesus.

In the midst of miracles, signs, and wonders, Jesus taught the people everywhere He went. Each time a miracle, a healing, or a deliverance took place, it was always while Jesus was teaching.

His teaching very largely consisted of illustrations or examples of some principle, some characteristic of God or of people, of the ways God operates and the ways the devil operates, and things that showed them the very nature of

1

the Father. Those illustrations are called *parables*. They are short stories of real-life situations that paint word pictures of the point He was making.

The woman with the spirit of infirmity came to Him as He was teaching in one of the synagogues on the sabbath day. (v. 10.) Teaching or preaching are prerequisites for receiving anything from God. If someone does not *hear* the Word, how can he be saved? (Rom. 10: 14,15.) Jesus knew that before people could properly be healed, delivered, or set free from sins, they must have His Word in their spirits.

John said that "the Word became flesh" and lived among men. (John 1:14.) So when the Word touches you, Jesus touches you. When the Word of God touches you, the *hand* of God touches you.

Another interesting thing you will see in the Gospels is that wherever Jesus taught, one or more people rose up against Him. In the midst of His conversations, someone always tried to find fault with what He was saying. How in the world Jesus walked in those synagogues and taught, I really do not know, because there was a teacher there already. The Jews called them "rabbis," and they were not the equivalent of our pastors, but they did lead the services.

However, the Bible says that Jesus taught with boldness and the kind of authority the rabbis did not manifest. (Matt. 7:29.) And many people listened to Him.

If you are now in a church where the Word of God is not being expressed in a fashion that ministers to body, soul, and spirit, then chances are *you are in the wrong church.* Not every building that has a cornerstone, a foundation, and a plumb line to designate the four corners is a "church." Brick and mortar, plywood and nails, or even stained glass and an organ or piano do not make that place a *church.*

The Church is made up of people, so a local church really means the body of people who meet there. The church meets *in* a building; it is *not* the building.

So many churches have been established with the right motives but somehow have gotten off center. Jesus must be the center of a church, not a tradition, doctrine, movement, teaching, or person.

Sometimes a preacher will walk into an already established church where the congregation is so dysfunctional that he cannot turn it. However, chances are, if the church is off, it is because the leader is off. If the leader is not hitting the target, no one in the house is going to hit the target.

Water comes from the top in a waterfall and flows downward. It does not run uphill. If the head is not right, how are you going to be right and stay right? Dysfunctionalism usually stems from the pastor and/or elders not being absolutely centered on Jesus. In the Jewish synagogues, the people and the rabbis were off center in Jesus' day. They objected to everything God was doing through Him.

Jesus was in a synagogue one sabbath when a woman arrived who had been afflicted with a spirit of infirmity for eighteen years, Luke wrote. What *is* a "spirit of infirmity"? A spirit is a created being who is invisible. Apparently there are many evil spirits in the supernatural realm that try to find people whose bodies they can share. Or they hunt those whom they can at least influence, oppress, or attack. So a spirit of infirmity is one that causes sicknesses or disease.

People are also spirits who live in bodies inherited from Adam and Eve. God created bodies for people to live in while in this material earth. Demons and angels do not have material bodies. Also, the Apostle John wrote that

God is a Spirit, and those who worship Him must worship Him in *spirit* and in *truth*. (John 4:24.) Jesus was a Spirit being who came to earth as a man in order to destroy the works of the devil. (1 John 3:8.)

Then there is another Spirit, the Holy Spirit, who was sent from God to dwell among mankind when Jesus ascended to Heaven. The Holy Spirit is to indwell those who are born again, and to become our Teacher, Counselor, and Friend. If we will listen to Him, He will guide and direct us into all truth.

If you are in a church where there is no love, chances are the Holy Spirit is not in charge there. Jesus said the world would know that His early followers were *His* disciples because they loved one another. (John 13:35.) The same should be true of us today. If God is not there, His Son is not there, and if the Son is not in a church, I know the Holy Spirit is not there either! Of course, the Godhead is present within those who are born again; however, the manifest presence of the Holy Spirit in the services and activities may not be there.

Where God is, people will praise His name, not to be seen of men and not to showcase great talent or musical knowledge of pitch and harmony, but from their hearts. When the heart is right, any cracks, squeaks, and missed words in the music are not really noticed. All you hear is the praise going forth.

Being in the wrong church can be a tragedy. I remember when I once found myself in the wrong church. I sat there knowing the pastor was preaching lies. I knew homosexuality was running rampant through the church and that the pastor could be considered "a whoremonger." The longer I stayed there, the farther from God I felt. All of my joy, all my strength, the presence of the Holy Spirit as the Anointer, and the power of God were being "zapped" from me.

However, every now and then, someone would sing a song from a genuine heart toward God, and I was able to endure. The song that usually struck a chord in my heart was titled "Jesus, the Center of My Joy." After a while, I began to search myself about where I was supposed to be. People looked at me "cross-eyed," unfriendly-like. If someone did not have on designer clothes and was not wearing diamonds, most of the others looked at that person as if he or she did not belong. If you were not driving a certain type of car, they would not fellowship with you.

The day that Luke writes about, Jesus must have been in a place like that. "Behold," Luke wrote, "there was a woman present who had a spirit of infirmity." The word *infirmity* indicates that she was physically weak. The infirmity actually had drawn the strength from her to the point where she was deformed.

Satan's Power Is Broken When Jesus Comes

She must have had a twisted vertebra, perhaps a slipped disc in the spine, or some kind of deformity that permeated her backbone all the way from the very top of her skull to the very tip of the lower lumbar region. This infirmity caused a curvature in her spine, which made her walk doubled over. The pain of this thing must have been excruciating.

The pain manifested in her face. She was in the wrong church bent over with pain. She was bowed over and could not lift herself up. I am sure that, as she hobbled around, she was a pitiful sight. And this did not occur because of sin in her life. Many people today still think that if you are going through some kind of suffering and tribulation, it is because you must be in sin. People think that because you are in a wheelchair, sin is the reason.

Some people think that you have to be beautiful, in perfect health, and have your life all together to come into God's house.

No, that is not true. Sometimes God permits you to go through things that will perfect your soul for the next part of your journey in His Kingdom. No matter what happens, however, you can be sure that when Jesus arrives on the scene, Satan's power is broken.

Have you ever heard someone say, "When I get some new shoes, or a suit, or a dress, I'm coming to church. When I get myself together, I'm coming to church," or, "When I get all my bills paid, I'm going to come to church and tithe."

The church is where you need to come to *get* it all together. This woman had the sense to go to the synagogue where she could hear the Word of God, although it may have been mixed with boring teachings that put her into slavery and condemnation. All those years, she sat there in her wretched condition and listened.

Then one day, Jesus came teaching, proclaiming Kingdom principles, and probably a praise song on His lips. In Biblical symbology, ten is the number of restoration and eight is the number of the resurrection. So *ten* and *eight* together equaled the number of years the woman had been afflicted. *Ten* registers that reconciliation and restoration were coming because Jesus was there, and eight is symbolic of resurrection. She needed to be "raised" out of her deadened condition.

We are in the same deformed, crooked condition when we come to Christ. In the natural realm, we may not show that kind of appearance; however, in the spiritual realm, we are deformed, brain damaged, and bowed down under the weight of our infirmities. We cannot see right, walk right, or talk right.

In Psalm 51:5, written after the prophet Nathan came to rebuke David because of his sin with Bathsheba, David's words of repentance were:

> **Behold, I was shapen** (molded, formed) **in iniquity, and in sin did my mother conceive me.**

The word *sin* in Hebrew is *chet* from the root of *chata*, which means "to miss"; hence, "to sin." The Greek word translated *sin* means "missing the mark." That means you came into the world with flaws, not perfect, not conforming to the way God created man in the beginning. You could not hit the target if you wanted to. You came into the world rebelling and deformed in spirit.

When you are in rebellion against God, you are the same as indulging in witchcraft. Men, when you function in rebellion, you are functioning in the spirit of a warlock. Women, when you rebel, you are operating in the spirit of witchcraft. (1 Sam. 15:23.)

Then David continued:

> **Behold, thou desirest truth in the inward parts: and in the hidden part** (the spirit) **thou shalt make me to know wisdom.**
>
> **Purge me with hyssop, and I shall be clean: wash me, and I shall be whiter than snow.**
>
> **Psalm 51:6,7**

Hyssop is an herb considered symbolic of the Passover lamb, because sprigs of it were dipped in the blood of the innocent lamb without spot or blemish and then brushed across the doorposts of the Israelites' homes. The death angel then "passed over" those homes when he came to take all the firstborn of the Egyptians. (Ex. 12:22,23.)

David was saying, "Wash me with Your blood, and I will be whiter than snow."

> **Make me to hear joy and gladness; that the bones which thou hast broken may rejoice.**
>
> **Hide thy face from my sins, and blot out all mine iniquities.**
>
> **Create in me a clean heart, O God; and renew a right spirit within me.**
>
> **Cast me not away from thy presence; and take not thy holy spirit from me.**
>
> **Restore unto me the joy of thy salvation; and uphold me with thy free (willing) spirit.**
>
> **Psalm 51:8-12**

David said, "Don't take Your Spirit away from me. I know I was born in sin and shaped in iniquity. I know I came here missing the target. But, Lord, please take Your blood and wash me so that I will be made whiter than snow.

"And, afterwards, create within me a clean heart. Renew a right spirit within me. Give me back my joy, the joy of Your salvation."

Turning away from serving the Lord will cost you the joy of His salvation, although it may not cost you your salvation. But it is a terrible thing to be saved and have no joy. The joy I have, the world did not give me and cannot take away. There is a joy deep in my soul.

I pray continually, "Father, wherever I go, I want Your Spirit to follow me and uphold me."

Salvation With No Joy Is a Terrible Thing

That woman with the spirit of infirmity must have

looked in the natural as we all look in the spirit before we are "raised" by Jesus to the life of God and transformed from the death of the fallen nature inherited from Adam. All of us are born bent over, crooked, undone, and missing the target. And there is nothing we can do about our conditions except ask the Lord to wash us with His blood.

He must give us a "transfusion," because the Bible says the life is in the blood. (Deut. 12:23.) When you have been washed clean and had a heart transplant, you can walk in the joy of His salvation and know His Spirit will indwell you and "follow" you all the days of your life in goodness and mercy. (Ps. 23:6.)

I am sure that the woman with the crooked back had been to doctors, who probably took all her money just like the woman with the issue of blood. (Luke 8:43) There was nothing doctors could do for those women. However, when Jesus came, all Satan's power was broken over them.

I look back over my own life and can say that I was really not a *bad* person. However, I was still crooked and bent over in the Spirit. I had pain until I met Jesus. When I met Him, a wonderful change came over me. I have never been the same. He straightened me up, fixed my spine, gave me a blood transfusion, and made my heart right.

When Jesus saw the woman, Luke wrote that He called her to Him. She did not go to the synagogue looking for healing. Her zeal for God caused her to be there in the right place at the right time. If she had not had a zeal for God, she probably would not have made herself attend synagogue in her physical condition. She would have been justified to remain home in bed. When Jesus called her, she had the faith to move out and walk up to Him in spite of her infirmity.

As she stood in front of Him, she was so bent over that she could not even look up into His face as He said,

"Woman, you are free of your infirmity." (v. 12.)

When He laid hands on her, Luke said that she *immediately* straightened up. The pain left, and her face lost its look of misery. And the first thing she did was glorify God. When you glorify God, you bless Him. She publicly acknowledged that a man named Jesus had touched her, and after eighteen years, she could stand straight and walk freely without pain. Blessed be the name of the Lord!

We ought not to be ashamed to let the world know where the Lord brought us from. We were bent over and ugly when Jesus touched us one day. Immediately, we straightened up and have never been the same. We ought to praise God so that the world will know His works. I am sure the woman did that the rest of her life.

She probably hunted for people to talk to, to say, "Just sit with me for a minute and let me tell you what a man named Jesus did for me. Just listen to me for a minute and let me tell you what God did for me. I used to be sick and afflicted. I was so bent over, I had to look down at the ground all the time. I was never free of pain, but this man named Jesus laid His hands on me and restored me to health."

You may be bent over as you read this. You may be crooked and deformed on the inside, but God can straighten you up through His Son, Jesus. When the Holy Spirit comes to you, Satan's power is broken. The Bible says that the anointing breaks the yoke. (Isa. 10:27.)

If you are in the wrong church, you probably are in a "dysfunctional" church, one that is off center in some fashion. The Lord began to show me some reasons why we are not functioning according to His will when I sought Him about the Body of Christ being ripped up, ostracized, and criticized in the past few years. The power of the Gospel has been diluted, and I asked the Lord to show me why this has happened.

I wanted to know what spirit is over this demonic activity that tears up a move of God when He is trying to do great things in the Body of Christ. And the Lord began to show me some things that cause dysfunction: things within Christians, within churches, and demonic activity that uses those things to tear up or hinder God's work.

In the next chapter, I want to talk about the kind of demonic spirit the Lord showed me is behind much of the chaos and turmoil taking place today in His Body.

2
Jezebel Spirits Also Manifest Through Men

Notwithstanding I have a few things against thee, because thou sufferest that woman Jezebel, which calleth herself a prophetess, to teach and to seduce my servants to commit fornication, and to eat things sacrificed unto idols.

And I gave her space to repent of her fornication; and she repented not.

Behold, I will cast her into a bed, and them that commit adultery with her into great tribulation, except they repent of their deeds.

Revelation 2:20-22

Before I begin to discuss this problem, I want to clarify some things that are being taught and believed in the Church today concerning "Jezebel spirits."

Satan does not care who he controls as long as he gets a body.

He is not a respecter of persons any more than God is: He just takes what he can get. A "Jezebel spirit" is one that causes someone, man or woman, to usurp the authority that rightly belongs to someone else of higher rank. That spirit causes the person it oppresses, influences, or possesses to get authority into his or her own hands.

These afflicted people pull strings, fill the role of the "power behind the throne," and generally take over. They manipulate, seduce, and deceive. The seduction is not always a physical thing, either. Sometimes it is an emotional seduction.

And the person who is "Jezebelic" can be a man as well as a woman!

Many churches, preachers, and Christians today have misinterpreted that scripture in Revelation. They have used it as a whipping tool to keep women out of the ministry. They have used the knowledge of spiritual things to hinder and even block God's will in moving some woman into a certain spiritual place.

They want to assume, and even state, that any time a woman comes forth in ministry, it is because of a "Jezebel spirit." Romans 10:15 says, **How beautiful are the feet of** *them* **that preach the gospel of peace,** and Paul did not say whether they were male or female feet. If you are carrying the Word of God - the good tidings that man has become reconciled with God (Col. 1:20) - then you are beautiful.

So if it is a Jezebel spirit, it could be over Johnny as well as over Mary. There are women with Jezebel spirits and men with Jezebel spirits. I have been in denominational churches where the pastors preached at women about "their" Jezebel spirits, when really those pastors, by oppressing women and suppressing the ministry of women, were themselves operating under "Jezebel spirits."

These spirits operate through control and domination. The Bible says that where **the Spirit of the Lord is, there is liberty** (2 Cor. 3:17), so wherever there is not liberty, you can be sure another spirit is in control. Our word *divination* comes from the Greek word for *python.*

In the book of Acts, the young woman who followed Paul and Silas around prophesying over them was said to have a "python spirit." In other words, she operated under a spirit of divination, which the apostles cast off her. (Acts 16:16-19.)

The Jezebel spirit is manifested through the spirit of divination, which I believe is one of the twelve strong men in the satanic network of rulers appointed to attempt to rule the systems of the world. (Twelve is the Biblical number that denotes government.) That means there are demonic strong men trying to rule, control, govern, and dictate the agendas of our lives and of society in every realm - educational, cultural, political, economic, and even religious.

Christians who are still "babes in the Lord," as Paul wrote to the Corinthians that they were (1 Cor. 3:1-3), are vulnerable to seducing spirits that can bind them and keep them out of the realm where God wants them to go. They are like children in the natural world, who are very vulnerable, because they do not have a depth of knowledge and experience of the world.

Take a boy or girl who runs away from home, goes to a new city, and gets off the bus cold and hungry with nothing to eat and nowhere to go. At that point, he or she is extremely vulnerable to the invitations of a pimp. Younger children, unless they are carefully taught and, in these days of evil, carefully watched over, can easily be coaxed into a car with a stranger on a promise of candy or some other treat.

If a Christian or a local or national church group does not recognize the authority they have in Christ, and if a nation does not acknowledge God's authority over it, one or more of Satan's strong men *will* govern in the spiritual realm and turn things more and more toward their foul plans. (Eph. 6:12.)

God Lives in the Hearts of His People

The "temple of God," individually and corporately, under the New Covenant, is made up of the spirits of His children. (1 Cor. 3:16.) The Father and the Son dwell in every born-again man, woman, boy, or girl in the Person of the Holy Spirit. In a corporate sense, the temple of God is the Body of Christ. As we meet together, we become the "visible Church." We are the outward representation of the "invisible Church" which is in the spiritual realm.

> **What? know ye not that your body is the temple of the Holy Ghost which is in you, which ye have of God, and ye are not your own.**
>
> **I Corinthians 6:19**
>
> **In whom ye also are builded together for an habitation of God through the Spirit.**
>
> **Ephesians 2:22**

There is another phase or stage of the Body of Christ, called "the Church Triumphant," and that is the one we are working toward and which Christians have been working toward for almost 2,000 years. We have not reached that place yet, but in Heaven, it is fixed. God sees it as already in place. He sees the battle already won.

In the natural realm, however, the Church Triumphant that we will be is yet being perfected in you and me. God has great things in store for us. His will is that we fulfill our destinies in Christ, and the only way to do that is to know our purposes, individually and corporately.

His purpose for you is His will for you, and you find the will of God through the Word of God. Once you find your purpose in order to fulfill your destiny, then you must know your proper season. You do not want to move out ahead of God and cast your fruit before its season. You do not want to "harvest" green, hard apples. Neither do you want to withhold your fruit until it is past time, when it becomes dried up or rotten.

The spirit of Jezebel will cause you to begin operating out of season. If you come forth too early, your ministry is premature and may be deformed, in some fashion off center, because everything about it was not yet formed properly. It has been birthed before its time. Also, when a baby comes too early, the chances of its dying are very high.

In the scenario briefly described by Jesus in Revelation 2, obviously a seducing spirit had crept into the church at Thyatira through a woman teacher. However, that does not mean it comes in through a woman every time, as I said earlier. False teaching comes from a "seducing spirit" that looks for minds open to it, no matter what race, nation, tongue, or sex.

In other words, false teaching involves a lie or lies that can seduce any mind that is *void of the deeper things of God.*

In chapters 2 and 3 of Revelation, Jesus was talking to seven churches in Asia Minor of which Thyatira was one. At the time the Apostle John received the visions and information written down in the book we call "the Revelation of Jesus Christ," he was imprisoned on the Isle of Patmos off the coast of Turkey, only a few miles from the church at Ephesus. John had pastored that church and had been banished for his testimony about Jesus Christ.

Patmos was a penal colony for criminals who worked in the mines and marble quarries of the ten-mile by ten-mile barren, rocky island. John, although around ninety years of age, probably received as rough a treatment as anyone else there.

Early church traditions and writings say that he was chained to a mule, which turned the equipment used in mining, and slept in a cave. A church has been built there commemorating the site. The stories say he was not even released from the mule at night and remained in bondage eighteen months. Then when the emperor who had imprisoned him died, the next one released prisoners who were not criminals. John was freed to minister several more years and write down the visions he saw on Patmos.

John found out what Jesus meant when He told the disciples that some of them would suffer as He had suffered. (John 15:20.) Suffering is a part of the lifestyle of those people of God who truly live separate from the world's society and represent Him as light and salt to the world. (Matt. 5:13,14.)

Not all of us are persecuted as some of the apostles were or as Christians have been in this century in the former Soviet Union and China. However, if you *truly* represent God, persecution from the world will come against you in some fashion. (Matt. 5:10,13:21.) But, we are supposed to live *above* circumstances, not under them.

And Satan does not care when he gets you as long as he gets you. You can praise the Lord until you are seventy-five, then backslide at seventy-five years and six months.

When I get old, I want to be wise. I want to be gray-headed and still walking around telling the truth about Jesus. The older you get, the more seasoned and power-ful in the Lord you should be. You should have deeper insights and be able to see farther than you could as a young Christian.

Older people who say, "Well, I've done all I can do now for the Lord, I'm just going to sit back and relax," are on the way out!

Some Christians look right in front of them when they should be looking down the road ahead. We should be visionaries. We should stretch our visions farther than our local churches and homes. We should look at other nations, especially at Third World countries, places where the Gospel is not preached extensively as yet.

God is looking for churches that are ready to expand and extend their visions and not be controlled and hindered by Jezebel spirits. Jezebel is strong and does not quit. It will choke the life out of a person or a church just as if they were caught literally in the coils of a python. A python will fall on your head and squeeze the life out of you, and that is what Jezebel spirits try to do.

Jezebel Perverts God's Purposes

The word *Jezebel* means "dung hill, an habitation of a dung hill." The word *dung*, of course, means "manure, excretion, or waste." A *dung hill* is dung mounded and piled up so that it gives off a stench, a stinking smell. The enemy wants to pull us into the habitation of waste and uselessness, so that we will become a stench in the nostrils of God.

But God wants us to be a "sweet-smelling savor" in His nostrils as Jesus was because of His love and willingness to lay down His life for mankind. (Eph. 5:2.) I am sorry to say there are few churches today that are on the mark with our Lord. If Jezebel is there anywhere, the Lord is not. If Jezebel is operating in a church, and the pastor is not dealing with it, then Jesus draws away. He will not compete.

Jesus will not force His way into our hearts, our lives, or our church groups. He must be invited in and welcomed. The Holy Spirit is easily grieved and must be ushered in. Jezebel shuts down the Spirit of God and causes everything done in that place to stink. If you are in tune enough with the Holy Spirit, sensitive enough to Him, you can walk into a place and actually smell something unclean. There is a sin of perversion that stinks, and when that demon comes out, it leaves an aroma, a trace.

There are sanctuaries in churches today that have become temples of idols instead of temples of the living God, all because of a spirit of Jezebel. That spirit must be dealt with in order for a church to become a beacon, a light, a powerhouse able to pull down strongholds for the move of God to go forth, for the very image to shine forth that God wants us to conform to, the image of Christ. Before that can take place, the image of Jezebel must be subdued.

Paul wrote in Ephesians 2:2 that Satan is the prince of the power of the air. He is in control of everything in the air — radio and television — and Christians must do spiritual warfare to get their programs through. If the enemy cannot keep us off the air, he hinders by attacking the tape equipment, the sound system, and every other way possible.

What do we see on television and in the movies today? Very little that is not violent, wicked, occult, perverted, and generally sinful. That is why Christians should monitor what their children see and hear, what toys they have, and where they go. Most popular music today opens up a door to Jezebel. Television tells you that everything from fornication to murder is okay.

Films and television set up nothing but scenarios and pictures in the souls (minds and emotions) of people that encourage and entice them to do things against God. The Jezebel attitudes of sensuality, witchcraft, and hatred of authority are running rampant in American society today. Jezebel spirits hate godly authority or even the natural authority of parents and governments. Jezebel wants to control and pervert all godly passions.

Some Christians want to be the best they can be for God. That is a godly passion. However, anyone who has insecurities, is jealous, or who moves in vanity and pride is a prime candidate for a Jezebel spirit. You can slip into vanity very easily in every realm of your life. Vanity can be very subtle about the way you look, the clothes you wear, or the way you walk and talk.

A person, man or woman, who has a particularly aggressive and domineering personality is very susceptible to Jezebel spirits. People who have codependencies, behavioral disorders, addictions, or strongholds of sin, unforgiveness, bitterness, and hatred are prime candidates for a Jezebel spirit.

I believe it is very important for everyone who reads this book to understand that all those operating under Jezebel spirits are *not* women. The world is also full of men who are vulnerable to Jezebel spirits. Everyone must guard his or her "temple" from invasion by the enemy in every way.

However, I must add that Jezebel spirits seem to attack women quicker. I believe that is because women deal in a lot of insecurities; and, to cover those up, they are prone to operate in a lot of vanity. That is why the Bible says a woman must put on the garment of meekness and quietness. (1 Pet. 3:4.) By doing that, no room is left for vanity.

Jezebel wants to be seen and heard. Jezebel wants to run things. Most women without Jesus, who are caught in relationships with abusive or dominating men, must open up to a Jezebel spirit to get free. Then the end results are usually worse than the first. They either end up in a similar relationship or are driven to use violence against the oppressor and end up in prison.

It was not the Spirit of God that led them out of those situations by putting on tight dresses and going out and getting new men. Jezebel spirits impart a survival instinct, a "talent" (ideas imparted by a demon) for escaping from bad situations. Jezebel spirits have ways of putting people under their influence in high places where they can subvert or pervert those in rightful authority.

Many preachers today cannot preach the unadulterated Word of God because they are living in adultery or living a life of lies in some other area. We have many dysfunctional men producing dysfunctional church members. All of them are missing the mark.

Jezebel Hungers After Earthly Power

"Jezebel spirits" are labeled that because they display all the characteristics of the woman named Jezebel, whose life is reported in 1 Kings. She was from Zidon, or Sidon, and was not the first woman from there to cause trouble in Israel. King Solomon took wives from the Moabites, Ammonites, Edomites, Zidonians, and Hittites. All of them worshiped a god called *Baal*, who was considered to be "lord of the harvest." He was a fertility god.

They believed that by engaging in sexual activity, which their god liked, he would bless the ground so that it would be fertile. Then they would have bumper crops. A goddess whose worship was parallel with Baal's was called Ashtoreth.

So part of the worship of this god and goddess involved sexual orgies and activities. Jezebel was high priestess of this cult in her day. In the Old Testament, seducing women were called "strange." (Prov. 2:16, 5:3, 7:5, and many other places.) In the New Testament, Christians are told to watch out for the seducing ways of strange women or men in a spiritual sense, those who preach strange doctrines. (Heb. 13:9.)

In 1 Kings 18 and 19, you will find the story of the original Jezebel and her encounter with the prophet Elijah. In 1 Kings 18:19, Elijah was ready to confront the prophets of Baal who had usurped God's authority over the ten-tribed nation of Israel because King Ahab had married Jezebel. (1 Kings 16:31.) As priestess of this pagan cult, she brought false prophets with her and supported them.

There were four hundred and fifty prophets of Baal and, in addition, there were four hundred "prophets of the groves" (places on high hills where fornication to the god took place). All of them ate at Jezebel's table, the Bible says. (1 Kings 18:19.)

It is a dangerous thing to eat at Jezebel's table. Her "table" is one that feeds you things you do not need. The spirit of Jezebel will feed you accusations, garbage, devouring things that will corrupt and contaminate your system, although it has already been purged by God. Before you know it, you will take on the same nature as the one at whose table you sit.

All of those priests were called to the top of Mt. Carmel to do battle with one man of God. The Jezebel always will try to stack the deck against a child of God. When God acts, the devil reacts.

How do you know if you are sitting with Jezebel? You can tell through the manifestations. If a dog brings a bone, he will take one and carry another. If you hear someone talking about other people, you can be sure that person will talk about you when you are not there. So you need to get away from Jezebel's table.

You can see from those chapters that God's one man whipped all of the hundreds of priests. That shows us that, although the odds may be stacked against us, we have authority, dominion, and power over the enemy. Greater is He that is in us than he that is in the world. (1 John 4:4.)

King Ahab went back to the palace with the promise of rain to end the three-year famine, but he also had to go back and tell Jezebel that all of her priests had been killed.

Then she sent a message to Elijah saying, "Let the gods do to me the same as you did to those men *if* I do not have your head by tomorrow at this time." (1 Kings 19:2.)

And what happened? The man who had just whipped 850 prophets rose up from his house and ran! A spirit threatened him, and he ran. Those spirits *will* threaten you. They never quit, if you do not cast them out. A demon put him to flight. He got out of God's will and fled to the wilderness, an area where he had no business.

God says to stand still and let Him fight the battle. (Ex. 14:13,14; Gal. 5:1; Eph. 6:13.) Then the victory will be yours. When you run, you always end up in uncharted areas. *Wilderness* means an unmapped, untamed area where Elijah more than likely had never been before. Whether he realized it or not, he was on the devil's ground. You can tell that is true because he sat down under a juniper tree and requested that he might die. (I Kings 19:4.) A spirit of suicide and absolute discouragement is not of God.

If you are flinching, fretting, worrying, grumbling and complaining, you are sending signals to the devil that you are scared. You can quote the verses about God not sending a spirit of fear and about being the head and not the tail all day, but if you are in fear underneath, the devil will know it. You are talking into the wind and shaking in your boots, not speaking forth the promises of God in faith.

Fear Opens the Door to Jezebel

Sometimes circumstances may push you back to the wall and make you think life is not worth living anymore. At that point, you need to understand that Jezebel has put a suicide spirit on you, and it is lying to you. Elijah had done great things the day before. Now he felt such discouragement that he thought God had failed! He thought he was the only one standing up for God until the Lord told him there were 7,000 more hidden away in Israel who had not bowed their knees to Baal.

The thing to do when you get discouraged is to edify yourself, encourage yourself by praying in tongues. When you need to pray and do not know what to pray, pray in tongues. That will edify you, and you will eventually move over into praise and worship. Then angels can go to work in your behalf.

As Elijah laid down to sleep, an angel touched him and said, "Arise and eat." (1 Kings 19:5-8.) So he ate, laid down and slept again, then the angel woke him to eat a second time. Even in his fear and discouragement, God had provided for him. Even when you do get out of God's will, He is still there. He will provide for you in the wilderness.

You may feel as if you have lost the battle from time to time, but you are not going to lose the war. It is already won!

God said, "Elijah, I have 7,000 who have not bowed their knees to Jezebel. You get back in there and put up a good fight for Me."

This point in Israelite history is where we get our name for these kinds of spirits. However, they manifested all through history even before that. They were manifesting when Moses' sister and brother rose up against him and proclaimed that God talked to them the same as He did to Moses. (Num. 12:2.) Family members often are your worst critics.

Shortly after Elijah killed the prophets and ran into the wilderness, something happened in Samaria, the capital of the northern Kingdom of Israel at that time. King Ahab decided he wanted a certain vineyard that belonged to a leading citizen, in whose family that land had been handed down since the tribes entered the promised land. (1 Kings 21:1-3.)

The owner would not sell it to Ahab, so he went back to the palace and pouted. His wife, in essence, asked him if he were a man or a mouse, and told him she knew how to get the land for him. (v. 7.) She wrote a letter under the king's name and seal to the neighbors of the man who owned the vineyard and had him killed through deception. (vv. 8-16.)

The spirit of Jezebel will kill if it needs to in order to win. It will kill you physically, or it may kill your reputation. Many in today's media are operating under Jezebel spirits. You can see the result in the damage being done to the reputation of some godly leaders. On the other hand, many Church leaders have allowed Jezebel spirits to cause them to sin and bring reproach on the Body of Christ.

Ahab thought he was discouraged because he could not get what he wanted; but really he was discouraged because he was under the control of his wife. Elijah became discouraged, not because he had failed God or failed to do God's will, but because he allowed fear to cause him to come under oppression to the spirit possessing Jezebel.

Elijah's life apparently was shortened because he ran from that spirit, but God wanted to keep His authority alive in the land. So He sent Elijah to pick his successor, Elisha. (1 Kings 19:16.) Then he allowed the prophet about ten years to train Elisha. Also, you can see that, at the same time, God pronounced sentence on Ahab and sent Elijah to anoint the man who was to be the next king (v. 16).

The mantle of Elijah has to be transferred through leadership. You do not get the Holy Spirit manifesting through you in the same way He did Elijah or even leaders of today simply by being saved. *Mantles* have to be transferred. If you want to be blessed with a double anointing, get behind someone who has the anointing.

At the end of his life, Elijah told Elisha, "If you see me when I go, you will receive a double portion of what I have." (2 Kings 2:9,10.)

Elisha wanted that very badly, so badly that he dogged Elijah's footsteps on that last day. He was with Elijah until he was taken up in a whirlwind, dropping his mantle to earth. The passing of Elijah's mantle to Elisha is a type and shadow of "a changing of the guard" in the spiritual realm.

The double anointing was so strong that Elisha turned around and immediately used the mantle to split the river in front of him. (2 Kings 2:13,14.) The mantle anointed by God has dominion and authority. So stop being fearful when satanist people begin bragging and boasting. Stop being fearful when Jezebel spirits attack well-known men of God.

The Holy Spirit wants to manifest in the land today as He did on Elijah. That "mantle" of anointing is resting only on those who have clean hands, pure hearts, and sanctified lives. If you have secret sins in the bunkers of your soul, you can forget about receiving that mantle. But, if you are willing to walk through places where many Christians do not go to receive the kind of power to call down fire *at God's command*, then keep holding on to the Holy Spirit.

When people have been blessed with that kind of "mantle," they can sing and pray a different kind of "fire" down from Heaven. People get saved, filled with the Holy Spirit, healed and delivered. Where did the fire of Elijah go? Where did the fire go that was given to Moses, Joshua, the judges, and the prophets?

In the Old Testament, you can trace the "mantle" of the Holy Spirit's presence: From Moses to Joshua to various judges, then to the prophets, and from Isaiah to Jeremiah to Ezekiel to Daniel. How many of us have that kind of anointing today?

No one who comes under the influence of Jezebel can receive the mantle of Elijah.

In the past, I have seen the spirit of Jezebel in operation and did not know what it was. Those kinds of spirits hang around or lay dormant until circumstances are right. Then you will see them rise up and try to take control. They wait until you get into a place where you have had defeat after defeat. Or they wait until men have no money and begin to suffer in their egos because they cannot be the bread-winners.

Other Characteristics of Jezebel Spirits

Under pressure, people may stoop and compromise, then Jezebel will rise up and take authority. Once ministers, in particular, lose their reputations, they are no more use to the Lord. You cannot allow those spirits to have *any* foothold in you.

You do not have to be consciously entertaining the spirit, but if there is a hole open in your mind, it can slip in. Once, years ago, there was a certain girl in the church that we were attending. Every time I turned around, she seemed to be there.

My wife would say, "Why do you keep looking at her?"

I would say, "I'm not looking at her," but my wife would reply, "Yes, you are!"

I had no desire for the girl, but she had desire for me. Because a door was open in me, the Jezebel spirit in her was beckoning to me.

I had to go to the Lord over the situation. Any time you do not know what is happening, it is a good idea to get into the Word of God and pray.

The Lord showed me there *was* a "hole" in me, and it was lust of the eyes.

He said, "You have subdued the lust of the flesh and the pride of life, but the lust of your eye is still there. And that is the area through which she is trying to control you, *My* preacher. And, if you do not get *your* eyes straight, you will not be able to be over any of My sheep."

He spoke to me just as clearly as I have ever heard, and when I lay down that night, He gave me a vision as a confirmation. I saw a round, black ball with power radiating all the way around it and permeating it. Then He showed me the ball with its entire area enclosed in a square except right in front.

He said, "Son, you are losing your power through the lust of your eyes. You have to get your eyes under the control of the living God."

I was losing the anointing. In other words, that spirit was about to box me in, so that the power of God could not radiate out.

Those spirits go after singers called of God, because they cannot fulfill their callings without the anointing. That spirit had lain dormant in me for years.

So I said, "Okay, Lord, why is it I have not been able to recognize what is happening until it is over or someone brings it to my attention?"

The Lord said, "Lust of the eyes is in your thought processes."

The spirit hides in the subconscious mind. The conscious mind then can honestly say, 'I'm not looking," while the subconscious says, "Look on, brother." So the devil was trying to hinder me by using images and thoughts that had been taken into my subconscious mind during my earlier life.

After that time of seeking the Lord, we went skating one night, and my wife said, 'Did you see her?

I said, "No, where is she?"

At that point, I had allowed the Holy Spirit to deal with the problem in my subconscious mind, and that spirit of enticement on her found no answering place in me.

I can tell you, reader, if you are called into the service of the Lord and you try to set forth without allowing these areas in your mind to be subdued, you could become a teacher of false doctrine.

When you teach true doctrine, it will condemn you. Instead of teaching the truth, you may be tempted to teach in error and lead people astray.

God said, "Woe to the pastors who scatter the sheep of My pasture. I will visit them." (Ezek. 34.)

Those pastors have a visitation coming, whether they want it or not. When the Lord says *woe*, it ought to get our attention.

The best way to keep the spirit of Jezebel off of you is to remain in a state of repentance. Otherwise, you build up an "immunity" to God. In the natural world, they give you an inoculation of measles vaccine so that you will not get measles. However, in God's world, it does not work that way. God does not give you sin so that you will not sin.

However, He will purge you through repentance. He will "shoot" repentance into your spirit and free you of any evil spirits. Presenting your body as a living sacrifice, holy and acceptable to God (Rom. 12:1), is the least you can do since Jesus went through the things He did to save you.

Furthermore, a spirit of Jezebel can be transmitted from generation to generation. The sins of the fathers become iniquities passed on to the children. If you do not break the power of those spirits that have been transferred to you, they will be transferred to your children, and then to theirs.

Entire lineages have become susceptible to demon possession because of this possibility. Have enough courage to get help if you feel some of these things are on you. When spirits fall away from you, depression leaves, sicknesses leave, and discouragement falls off. You will begin to get some victories in Jesus, and your children can grow up to be what they are destined to be in God.

Until you get generational curses off you, nothing major for God will happen in your life. You must lose yourself to find God. God is a good God, and He can do anything but fail. If there is any failure, it is in us. God Himself said that we are defeated because of lack of knowledge. (Hos. 4:6.) In other words, we fail because we do not have enough of His Word in us to discern truth and falsehood.

In the next chapter, we are going to look at how to discern false prophets, those who preach strange doctrines or whose motives in preaching the truth are something besides serving God and being called according to *His* purpose. False prophets have their own agendas and cause people and churches not to function properly in God's will.

3

Discerning False Prophets

Now concerning spiritual gifts, brethren, I would not have you ignorant.

1 Corinthians 12:1

So many Christians are ignorant of spiritual gifts, even today after almost a century of living in a time when those gifts have been restored to the Body of Christ. Many Christians have knowledge of physical things, intellectual things, and even of the Bible; yet, they remain essentially ignorant about the spiritual gifts.

I want to specifically discuss "the gift of prophecy." (1 Cor. 12:10.) I want to show you how to receive a prophecy and how to discern prophecies, whether or not they are of God. If someone gives you a prophecy that you feel in your spirit is right, should you sit down and wait for it to come to pass? Or should you be running around trying to fulfill it?

In the Nineties, when the office of prophet is being more and more accepted and is being restored to the Body of Christ, it is more important than ever to be able to tell what is of God, what is of a familiar spirit, and what is simply coming from the person's own thinking. Not every prophecy is of God. Everyone who comes with a "yabba dabba doo" is not of God.

Perhaps you have been prophesied over by many

people. Perhaps you have been told that you are going to be wealthy, but you cannot even find a job.

Perhaps you have been told you are to have a great ministry, and you wonder why you are not being sent forth.

Perhaps you have been told you are going to find a husband or a wife and do great things in the spiritual realm, yet you cannot even seem to get a date.

Let's look first at the rest of Paul's description of spiritual gifts:

> Now there are diversities of gifts, but the same Spirit.
>
> And there are differences of administrations, but the same Lord.
>
> And there are diversities of operations, but it is the same God which worketh all in all.
>
> For the manifestation of the Spirit is given to every man to profit withal.
>
> For to one is given by the Spirit the word of wisdom; to another the word of knowledge by the same Spirit;
>
> To another faith by the same Spirit; to another the gifts of healing by the same Spirit;
>
> To another the working of miracles; to another prophecy; to another discerning of spirits; to another divers kinds of tongues; to another the interpretation of tongues:
>
> But all these worketh that one and the selfsame Spirit, dividing to every man severally as he will.
>
> **1 Corinthians 12:4-11**

The "gifts," or manifestations of the Holy Spirit through some person to the Body of Christ, can be divided into three kinds of supernatural manifestations:

1. *Revelation gifts* (words that reveal things): word of knowledge, word of wisdom, discerning of spirits.

2. *Inspirational gifts* (words that warn or inspire): prophecy, divers kinds of tongues, and interpretation of tongues.

3. *Power gifts* (manifestations that literally *do* something): faith, miracles, and healings.

As I said, however, I want to concentrate on the gift of prophecy in this chapter. Before we can talk about prophecies, we need to understand the difference between the office of a prophet and a person who operates in the Holy Spirit's gift of prophecy. Not everyone who prophecies is a prophet. The Holy Spirit *could* use someone to bring forth a prophecy one time, yet never again.

The *gift* is to the believer. The manifestations of the Holy Spirit in these nine ways are presents to the Body of Christ. It is a mistake to think of *gift* in these verses as being synonymous with *talent*. These are not talents or abilities given to certain people; they are presents to individuals or local groups of Christians manifested *through* someone who is willing to be so used.

However, the *Holy Spirit* chooses the ones He wishes to use as vessels of communication (v. 11.) You cannot earn the opportunity. However, you can pray to be so used (v. 31.) and submit yourself to the Holy Spirit to be used.

Many people tend to take for granted the privilege of being so used by the Holy Spirit. Others desire (are ambitious for status or crave attention) the things that being used by the Spirit brings to the extent that they push themselves forward and give words out of their mind. They present things they already know as "a word from God." Still others are influenced by familiar spirits so that they give forth false prophecies and, sometimes, do not even know the words they speak are not of God.

Those of us who walk in the office of prophet or are used by the Holy Spirit to deliver His manifestations to other people need to understand that we are stewards of a high calling in Christ Jesus. We need to watch ourselves for signs of pride and make every effort to manifest the fruits of the Spirit (Gal. 5:22,23) and remain humble. We need to understand clearly that we are vessels, not the treasure contained *in* the vessels.

Jesus said that we will give account for every idle (non-working) word that comes out of our mouths. (Matt. 12:36.) If your heart is right, you will not get into error, but you will speak forth truth. A true prophet is one who knows truth revealed from God and speaks it forth, an inspired person who proclaims the Word of God to others.

Prophets also may be used of the Holy Spirit as "seers," those who are given knowledge of future things.

The Difference Between True and False Prophets

A true prophet will not be able to keep his mouth shut when the words of God rise up in his spirit. Jeremiah, a prophet to Judah in the last days of that nation, found this out as a literal truth. He told the Lord that, because people hated and persecuted him when he spoke forth the words of God, he tried not to speak. But, Jeremiah said, the words of God burned in him like fire and *had* to come out. (Jer. 20:7-9.)

Not just prophets but preachers and teachers can get in the place Jeremiah found himself. They can get discouraged and depressed and not want to go tell someone the things the Holy Spirit wants them to say. But the words of the Lord will be like fire shut up in their bones, and sooner or later, they will have to deliver the message of the Lord.

A prophet is a special agent of God raised up to proclaim the words of the Lord. Jeremiah was called from his mother's womb, according to God's word to him. (Jer. 1:5.) True prophets will not compromise. Jeremiah tried to get out of delivering the messages of God, but when he did deliver one, he made no compromises.

So one way you can tell a true prophet is if that person does not compromise. A person who changes what he says, changes directions in the Lord, and softens the word of God is compromising.

A false prophet is someone who does not see and does not speak truth. Those who start out on the right path with every intention of working for Jesus can get into error if they do not discern that certain words are from their own minds or from false spirits. They become false teachers or false prophets.

A false prophet is one who speaks lies, compromises with the uncompromising Gospel, and makes exceptions for "special" people (ones who can give him some advantage in the natural, or who have money to donate), instead of dealing across the board with everyone on the same level. He would rather do the work of the ministry for money, or he is yet indulging in the things of the flesh, living as a carnal man, not realizing that he has erred.

Prophets also can get so spiritually arrogant that they become pompous and full of pride. Then they slide into being false prophets. They have an answer for everything. When they are not anointed by the Holy Spirit's presence any longer, they begin to make up words and people are lead astray.

A false prophet will give words that pacify the flesh and weaken the spirit, while a true prophet will call you to repentance. He will instruct you, correct you, motivate you, and activate what is in you. A false prophet will *not* activate the gifts within you, because if he thinks your administration of a spiritual gift will give you authority over him, he wants to keep you down.

False prophets will not let women teach, preach, or get in the pulpit. They want to control women and keep them under their thumbs.

Instead of motivating you, they suppress gifts and try to deactivate you.

I am reminded of a message I heard a long time ago called, "The Eagle Stirs the Nest."This preacher explained that when it comes time for little eagle to fly, the mother eagle stirs the nest from time to time. When she does, at least one of the youngsters will get pushed out of the nest. If the little bird's wings do not spread, the mother would swoop down, catch it, and bring it back to the nest.

The mother stirs the nest until all of the eagles are able to fly, move in the air, and float as adults.

The Church needs to mount up with wings as an eagle. We need to learn how to fly in the things of God, because I believe we are coming to a time that Christians will starve if they are locked into staying on the ground and eating bird seed provided for them. The "deep" things of God, the highest level of spiritual things, will only come to you if you learn how to fly in the Spirit. Many Christians have been in their nests too long.

That does not mean I am saying to jump out and start your own church or ministry. What I am saying is to take the strength you have gained in the Lord so far and go out and help strengthen someone else.

If Christians understood the seriousness of being chosen as a steward over one of the five-fold offices or over one or more of the operations of the Holy Spirit, they would be much more careful about handling the things of God. If everyone understood the *accountability* to God that goes with these things, he or she would be extremely quick to give forth the messages of God and extremely careful to make sure that those messages *are* of God and that their motives are right.

Do you get things through "vain imaginations"? (Rom. 1:21; 2 Cor. 10:5.) Then you will be held accountable for the blood of those who are misled. Their blood will be on your hands. This kind of false prophet leads people by his or her own understanding of things, not by the Word of God, and the motivation may not be intentionally to move people away from God. Some things this kind of person says *may* fit the Word of God taken out of context.

A false prophet of whatever kind will say things from time to time, however, that do *not* line up with the Bible. A true prophet always will speak forth those things that are confirmed by the written Word of God. All of the major and minor prophets of the Old Testament days pointed to the *one* true prophet: Jesus Christ.

False prophets, who lead people away from the things of God through spirits of divination (the python/Jezebelic spirits of the last chapter), do so by intent of the demon, if not knowingly by their own intention. Those who attempt or pretend to operate in supernatural things out of greed or ambition may not set out to intentionally draw people off the right path, but at the very least, they do not *care* about other people. As long as they get monetary gain, it does not matter to them if they cause you to stumble.

People today are so hungry for the things of the Spirit and not getting the right things that they have become infatuated with the supernatural. Palm readers, astrologers, and fortune tellers are more popular today than they have ever been, and you can find their offices all over the place, even next door to churches.

It is a dangerous thing to stand up and prophesy in the name of Jesus and not be speaking truth. God said the prophet that "presumes" to speak a word in His name that He has not commanded that person to speak shall die, just as a person who prophesies in the names of other gods. (Jer. 23:13-17.) Even those who begin to prophesy out of their own minds, thinking it is God, are in great danger. Their deception, for whatever motive, places them squarely into the occult camp. If they do not have familiar spirits, they very easily can acquire them.

Sometimes people with Jezebelic spirits use prophecy to control other people. They threaten and cause fear through supposedly prophetic words.

Testing Prophecies

In order to discern false prophets, you must have a clear channel to the Holy Spirit. You must get out of the flesh: out of what you believe, what you see, or what you feel. *Discernment* is not matching what is said against what you believe or already know. You might have the wrong beliefs or the wrong information.

You must match what is said against the Word of God. Be like the people at Berea, who "searched the scriptures daily" to see if the apostles were speaking truth or were false prophets. (Acts 17:11.) In addition to that, there is a "witness" in your spirit to truth if you are sensitive to the Holy Spirit. He will give you an answer in your spirit so that, although you may not clearly understand what was said as yet, you will "know that you know" it was true.

He ordinarily will not give you an answer in your mind, just a "knowing" of truth or falsehood. Then it is up to you to go to the Bible and check it out, so that your mind has a knowledge of *why* that thing was true or false.

If you remain ignorant of spiritual things, you will not be able to walk in an attitude of discernment. Speaking in tongues edifies and builds up your spirit man. It is a good way to build the relationship between you and the Holy Spirit to a point where you are aware of His witnessing and His guidance through a sense of peace or a lack of peace.

If you want victory in your life in any area, get out of the flesh. Flesh will rise up and give you "itching ears" and eyes blinded to the things of God. (2 Tim. 4:3.)

When you find yourself in a place where you cannot "hear" in the Spirit, say to yourself: "Wake up!"

Another standard to use in judging prophecies is 1 Corinthians 13:9. Paul wrote that we know in part and prophesy in part. In other words, no one has the whole truth or the entire picture, only the part the Holy Spirit chooses to bring forth through you. So if anyone comes to you with a lengthy description of your life in the past and what God is going to do in the future, it probably is not God — although the Holy Spirit could do that if He wanted to.

My point is that, as His nature and character are shown forth in the Bible, He more than likely would not do that. Although the woman at the well ran back to Samaria saying that a Man had told her all she had ever done, she really meant He had told her how many men with whom she had been involved and the marital status she had been in with each one, not literally *everything* she had done. (John 4:29.) Jesus never disclosed to her details of her entire Life.

God does not change. (Heb. 13:8.) He does the same things He has done since creation. God does not "show off." He does not have to. Anything supernatural that the Holy Spirit manifests is for a purpose, for a reason, not simply to be spectacular.

If someone is prophesying over you and going through all of this carnival-like stuff that detracts from the awareness of the presence of the Holy Spirit and distracts attention away from Jesus, you can discern that operation is not of God. In those instances, flesh is getting the glory, not God.

Usually the Holy Spirit only shows you a glimpse, a hint of direction, to encourage you to keep on working, to answer questions that you have sought the Holy Spirit about, or to build your faith in order that you may receive something He has for you. If everything were told you all at once, there would be no room for *faith*. And God said that without faith, it is impossible to please Him. (Heb. 11:6.)

Most of us could not handle it if God were to reveal the things He wants to do with our lives. From where we are at any given point, future things would seem so awesome we would lose heart of ever getting there, or we might start off trying to get there in our own ways, our own timings, and our own works.

Revelation 1:10 tells of John seeing Jesus on the Isle of Patmos. But first, he saw an angel, at whose feet he tried to fall and worship.

But the angel said, "Don't do this! I'm just a servant like you and your other brethren who have the testimony of Jesus. Worship God, for the testimony of Jesus is *the spirit of prophecy.*"

That says that all prophecy involves testifying of Jesus or is to accomplish things that *will* testify of Jesus. When we move in the gifts of the Spirit or operate in any of the five-fold offices under a true anointing, we are moving with the Holy Spirit to point to and glorify Jesus, and through Him, the Father, and to inspire others to do the same.

True prophecy is an utterance from the throne room of God. That means that, if you want to prophesy, get filled with the Holy Spirit and seek to get close to the Father and the Son.

If you have a testimony of Jesus that is, beyond the shadow of a doubt, untarnished with sin, out of your "belly" (spirit) will flow the rivers of living water that originated in Jesus. (John 7:38.) Those rivers include prophetic words. You will speak truth.

Many times, there are more false prophets than true. Look at Israel in the days of Elijah.

And, in earlier times, Babylon was headquarters for soothsayers, or false prophets, and there were many more of them than there were of God's men. Also, the pharaoh of Egypt had several soothsayers to face Moses, God's prophet. (Ex. 7:11.)

How To Receive Prophecy

Concerning what you do with prophecies, you need to know there are three kinds of true prophecies: partial, progressive, and conditional.

There are prophecies that give you only a part of an event or happening, or perhaps, only the next step in your path, not the entire path. Others will come true, or be fulfilled step by step, although you are given the picture all at once. Prophecies of Messiah are of the first two kinds. Some were partial pieces of the whole picture, and others were of a progressive nature.

No prophecy about Jesus, however, was of the third kind of prophecy. This third category involves prophecies that are *conditional* on your choices and actions, or on someone else's.

The book of Jonah gives us a detailed, exact example of this last kind of prophecy. Whether or not God's pronouncement of doom came true depended on the choices of the king and residents of Nineveh. In other words, Jonah's message from God was "conditional."

Prophecies of Jesus' coming, however, were fixed. No human being's choices had anything to do with His first coming. God determined His Son was to come to earth, and He spoke that forth as a matter of fact.

So, suppose you have a discernment that a word to you really is of God. You have tested it by His written Word, and it has passed the test. The person giving it was a person showing good fruit of the Spirit who gave you the word in a righteous and humble manner. Now what do you do with that word?

The first thing to do with a prophecy given you is write it down as exactly close to what the prophet said as possible. Make sure you do not write down what you think he, or she, *meant*. You might have misunderstood or misinterpreted. Get the exact words, if at all possible. Get the tape, if the word came to you in a service that was being taped, and play it again and again.

Then check it with the Bible, and pray over it in tongues until you have a clear witness one way or the other from the Holy Spirit.

An important thing of which to be aware is that, if you receive a true prophecy, *your flesh may immediately reject it.*

So an immediate reaction, whether it is against a prophecy or for it, needs to be laid aside in favor of the kind of discernment showed us in the Bible. You must be open to an anointing of your spiritual eyes and ears by the Holy Spirit in order to truly receive an anointed word.

If a word is from God, your soul usually wants nothing to do with it. Why? Because a true word from God, in a direct prophecy or an indirect message from the pulpit, a book, or a television message, will come against, or confront, everything in you that is *not* of God. So the flesh brings up a strong defense against it.

Once you are sure the word is of God:

• Begin to meditate on that word in order for the Holy Spirit to give you a proper understanding of what it means and of the timing He has in mind for it.

• Set your trust in Him to show you anything you need to do in bringing that thing to pass.

• But, also, set your flesh *not* to do anything about that prophecy without a clear witness from the Holy Spirit.

Beware if you hear prophecy or preaching that puts forth the idea that it is all right to do some sins even if not others. I have heard of prophecies that told a wife to leave her husband for another man, or a husband to leave his wife for another woman. That is a prophecy that tells you not only is it okay to commit adultery but that God is telling you to! That is positively opposite to the written Word of God.

On the other hand, it also is a dangerous thing to override a true prophet of God or to refuse to receive a word from God to or for you. Look what happened to the prophets of Baal and, eventually, to Ahab and Jezebel for standing against God and coming against His prophets.

First John 4:1 says that, in the apostle's own day, "many" false prophets already had gone out into the world. He wrote that Christians definitely are to *try* the spirits to see whether they are of God. John gave another way to test prophecy, teachings, or messages:

> **Hereby know ye the Spirit of God: Every spirit that confesseth that Jesus Christ is come in the flesh is of God:**
>
> **And every spirit that confesseth not that Jesus Christ is come in the flesh is not of God: and this is that spirit of antichrist, whereof ye have heard that it should come; and even now already is it in the world.**
>
> **1 John 4:2,3**

How To Be Used in the Gifts

If you want to be used by the Holy Spirit in the gifts, you need to deal with any areas of your past where you have dabbled in the things of the occult. Those include the New Age movement, astrology, reflexoloy, fortune telling, tarot cards, and any other thing listed by Moses as the demonic supernatural and not to be tolerated by people of God. (Deut. 18:10-14.)

If you have ever been involved in any of those things, including taking part in seances or using the ouija board or pendulum-discerning, you need to stop reading right now and denounce those things. You must genuinely repent of being involved in sinning against God by participating in supernatural operations that are counterfeits of His operations.

Leviticus 20:6 says:

> **And the soul that turneth after such as have familiar spirits, and after wizards, and go a-whoring after them, I will even set my face against that soul, and will cut him off from among his people.**

So you see it is as dangerous to run after false prophets as it is to become one. The Lord wants us to set ourselves apart from that kind of foolishness, from those things that pretend to be of Him but really are following "strange" gods (demons). Those things will pollute your spirit, even if you do not become totally involved. Reading occult material will darken your mind to the things of God.

In Deuteronomy 13:1-5, Moses warned the Israelites not to follow after "prophets" or "dreamers of dreams" who did signs and wonders or prophesied signs and wonders that came to pass. That shows that false prophets can have powers from demons to do lying wonders that can be strong delusions.

A false prophet is a liar, and a false prophecy is a lie, no matter who gives it or what motive that person has. And lying is one of the things that God hates. Anything God hates is an extremely serious thing.

4
God Hates Lying

These six things doth the Lord hate: yea, seven are an abomination unto him:

A proud look, a lying tongue, and hands that shed innocent blood,

An heart that deviseth wicked imaginations, feet that be swift in running to mischief,

A false witness that speaketh lies, and he that soweth discord among brethren.

Proverbs 6:16-19

When God hates something, that is serious! David said God hates all "workers of iniquity." (Ps. 5:5.) In this chapter, however, I only want you to look at one of the things He hates: lying. If you want to make God mad, let your mouth start running with things that are not true.

There are so many lies being hissed today, and I say "hissed" because anyone who lies has the tongue of a snake. There is hissing from pulpits, hissing on the radio and television, and hissing in private from people teaching and propagating lies.

The father of lies is Satan, and if you lie all of the time, who is your father? Satan is your father. Jesus talked about this fact with the Jews of His day.

. . . If God were your Father, ye would love me: for I proceeded forth and came from God; neither came I of myself, but he sent me.

49

> Why do ye not understand my speech? even because ye
> cannot hear my word.
>
> Ye are of your father the devil, and the lusts of your
> father ye will do. He was a murderer from the beginning,
> and abode not in the truth, because there is no truth in him.
> When he speaketh a lie, he speaketh of his own: for he is a
> liar, and the father of it.
>
> And because I tell you the truth, ye believe me not.
>
> Which of you convinceth me of sin? And if I say the
> truth, why do ye not believe me?
>
> John 8:42-46

From the very beginning, the devil has had a sinister plan to birth disciples into the world. Satan has disciples, did you know that? The Greek word for *disciple* simply means a "learner."

If you are a disciple of Christ, you are one who learns of Him. You have tasted and seen that the Lord is good. (Ps. 34:8.) You have taken up your cross daily to follow Him. (Mark 10:21.)

Likewise, there are people totally engrossed in wickedness. They constantly devise evil things to destroy God's creations. They have learned the art and tactics of Satan worship and today's form of the "deep things" of Satan, which is called New Age. These people have become learners (disciples) of Satan.

Satan chooses his "preachers" just as Jesus, the Head of the Church, chooses those to represent Him in what we call the five-fold offices: apostle, prophet, evangelist, pastor, teacher. God's servants of righteousness are called, touched, and chosen by the hand of God. Likewise, the devil steadily picks and chooses those who will deliver his messages of unrighteousness, hissing lies, and vulgarities to draw people into his kingdom.

As surely as God has chosen me to proclaim righteousness, holiness, living above your circumstances, and walking in prosperity, the enemy has chosen another person to go around in my area preaching against what God is saying through me. If you do not realize that is true, you are not living in the real world.

Satan has a sinister plan to pervert understanding of God's Word. If he can pervert, distort, or confuse your understanding of the Bible, he can keep you from having an accurate picture of Who Jesus is, Who God is, and Who the Holy Spirit is. His plan is behind the media's concerted effort to make God's people look stupid or worse.

I do realize that some leaders in the Church have allowed sin to run rampant in their lives, so that reproach has been brought on the Church and the Kingdom of God. However, everything that is "exposed" is not true. Much "hissing" is going on out there against even righteous men and women of God.

The Spirit of the Living God is saying that His people must begin to truly respect His anointed leaders. I am not talking about preachers who are living a lie, but about those who are pulling down demonic strongholds, laying hands on the sick, and teaching the Bible without adding or subtracting from it.

God hates liars, and there *are* some preachers out there pretending to be doing signs and wonders that really amount to fakery. They find out all about people, then get in the service and pretend to be operating in spiritual gifts. If you truly have God within you, you cannot lie because *God cannot lie*. (Titus 1:2.)

The Holy Spirit Is the Spirit of Truth

The Holy Spirit, on the other hand, is the Spirit of truth. Jesus told His disciples that when the Holy Spirit came to earth, He would guide them (and, by inference, all disciples of Christ thereafter) into all truth. (John 16:13.)

The Holy Spirit does not speak of Himself, but of Jesus, and He will show us things to come, Jesus said.

If a person truly is empowered by the Holy Spirit, there will be no "I," "me," or "my." Someone walking in the Spirit of truth will not be saying, "I built this church," "I really preached today," or similar things that focus on self. The Holy Spirit glorifies Jesus and the Father. If you are doing a holy dance, and God is not getting the glory, but attention is focused on you, then you are glorifying yourself.

A lot of people have believed a lot of lies, and because they believed those lies, they became partakers in the deception put forth by lying demons. A liar cannot hang onto the truth. People with a spirit of lying will not be able to hang around where truth is being spoken. They will be offended.

A preacher or teacher moving in the Holy Spirit preaches to the spirits of the people. But many in the congregation hear in the flesh and get offended. The same people will receive something said that "strokes" the flesh. Just because someone drives a big car, wears a three-piece suit, and can speak in great platitudes or snappy cliches does not mean that person is speaking truth.

If you have the Spirit of truth inside you and are truly submitted to His authority, nothing but truth will come out of your mouth. Why? Because you have God in you, and God cannot lie. (Titus 1:2.)

How do you get the Spirit of truth to dwell within you? To receive the Holy Spirit, one of two things must happen: you must surrender and open the door to your heart, or you must have been so broken by circumstances that you are open to Him.

Sometimes people have to be bruised by the devil

before they come to the realization that Jesus is Lord and their ever-present help in time of trouble. (Ps. 46:1.)

Some people cannot believe in God, because they have their eyes fixed on natural things, and God is a Spirit. Jesus and the Holy Spirit are spirits. The devil and his demons and fallen angels are spirits. Inside these bodies of flesh, people are spirit beings. The supernatural realm is the eternal one. The flesh world decays and will pass away. But many people have trouble seeing past the flesh and past things made of natural matter.

Jesus told the disciples about the Holy Spirit in John 14 and 16:

> And I will pray the Father, and he shall give you another Comforter, that he may abide with you for ever;
>
> Even the Spirit of truth; whom the world cannot receive, because it seeth him not, neither knoweth him: but ye know him; for he dwelleth with you, and shall be in you.
>
> John 14:16,17

The Holy Spirit is not someone you can see. He is a spirit, but the people of this world say, "We need to see Him, or we will not believe."

Can you see the wind? Yet it is there.

Can you see your blood or your brain? Yet, you know your brain and your blood are there.

You may say, "Yes, but we can see manifestations of blood and brains."

If you will look, you can see manifestations of the Holy Spirit as well. I am not referring only to signs, wonders, miracles, healings, and the gifts of the Spirit. I am talking about holiness, about people who live sanctified lives in the image and pattern of Jesus, about people who walk in love.

Jesus told His disciples:

> I will not leave you comfortless: I will come to you.
>
> Yet a little while, and the world seeth me no more; but ye see me: because I live, ye shall live also.
>
> . . . If a man love me, he will keep my words: and my Father will love him, and we will come unto him, and
>
> make our abode with him.
>
> He that loveth me not keepeth not my sayings: and the word which ye hear is not mine, but the Father's which sent me.
>
> These things have I spoken unto you, being yet present with you.
>
> But the Comforter, which is the Holy Ghost, whom the Father will send in my name, he shall teach you all things, and bring all things to your remembrance, whatsoever I have said unto you.
>
> John 14:18,19,23-26

There is *one* Lord — Father, Son, and Holy Spirit — regardless of what some religions and even Protestant denominational cults say. There are not three Gods, but One. Paul wrote that there is one Body (or one Church), one Spirit, one Lord, one faith, one baptism, and one God. (Eph. 4:4-6.) From the bosom of God came Jesus, born on earth as a man, born of a virgin — all God and all man. He walked and lived in the flesh, yet He knew no sin. The Word became flesh, John wrote, and dwelt among mankind. (John 1:14.)

Before Jesus departed earth to return to the Father, He spoke of a Comforter. To have left His disciples without the presence of God would be to have left them - and all of us since — "comfortless." Mankind, before Jesus, was comfortless, with the exception of those in covenant with God through Abraham.

The indwelling Holy Spirit brings truth and reality to our lives, and lying is a process that takes the reality and the assurance of truth out of life. Lying distorts the living process of a Christian life. It keeps you from living in tune with your own spirit. It keeps you from living in tune with the Holy Spirit. It is virtually impossible to be in tune with God and not be in tune with yourself.

If you do not know who you are, where you came from, and what you as a person are all about, it is virtually impossible for you to come into the right relationship with Jesus Christ. If you are not in tune with the Holy Spirit through you own spirit being, it is virtually impossible to move in integrity, morality, and spiritual awareness.

However, once you admit that you are wretched and no good, and that everything about you is of the world because you are practicing the things of the world, then there is hope for you. When you stop lying to yourself and admit that your life is contrary to God's Kingdom, then you are in a place to truly receive Jesus or to truly walk as a follower and disciple of Him.

You have no morals or ethics when you live under the world's system of thinking, because the world says anything is all right under certain circumstances. The world has no absolute standard of right and wrong. You can adjust your morality to the situation. But, my friend, *that is lying.*

If you do not have the Holy Spirit, then He cannot lead and guide you to truth. He is the One Who leads us to Jesus. You need the Holy Spirit for everyday living as well as indwelling truth, so that you will recognize truth when you hear it and lies when you hear lies. God's ways are opposite to the world's ways, and much of even Christians' time and attention goes to things of the devil because they do not have discerning spirits.

Three Levels of Lying

There are three levels of lying: You lie to yourself, then you lie to others around you, and finally, you lie to the world, to everyone. Some people have progressed to the point that they are "compulsive liars." They will tell a lie for no reason, simply because they can no longer tell the truth.

At that point, a person's whole life is nothing but one big lie. Once you start lying to yourself, you lose touch with who you are. Then you are out of touch with God, out of touch with family and friends, and out of touch with employers and pastors.

At the next level, you begin to lie to people around you, usually beginning with your spouse. Many times, lying comes from a fear of authority. Some folks fear authority so much, they will lie to keep from having to deal with authority. The characteristic that manifests after a deep involvement in lying is *deceit*. That means those people cannot be trusted in any area, usually because they have come under the influence of a lying spirit, at that point.

I dislike a cheat and a liar. I will not say *hate*, because I am not God, but I really dislike people with these characteristics. Exaggerating a "good story" is a lie, no matter what you call it. People trying to make themselves look better by lying are operating in vanity and pride.

Some people simply lie to be lying. If you are a habitual liar, you are out of touch with reality. You are at the point where it is impossible for you to be honest. Your integrity was tried by the spirit of lying and found wanting.

A lying spirit develops in three phases:

1. The first phase begins with thoughts, a thought process given you in the way the demon wants you to speak it forth.

2. The second phase is when you begin to believe what you hear. You have become conditioned to falsehoods.

3. The third phase is when you begin to cause others to believe lies. When you tell a lie, you are allowing a demon to actually speak through you, using your voice, your body, which as a Christian, is the temple of God. Once you speak the lie, you become a liar. Lying from then on is an ongoing action of the first lie. A liar plus fluent lying equals a professional "con man."

A "con man" knows what to say and when to say it so that he will be believed and his lies not found out. People who believe his lies will be cheated, seduced, or even worse. A "con man" is fathered by the devil and is a disciple of the enemy.

Christians have been lied to today so much that many of them think that someone who looks good, is well-groomed, and speaks eloquent words is a preacher to be listened to. So some pastors allow certain men and women to stand in their pulpits and minister hissings to the sheep for which they are responsible and accountable. Some pastors expose their sheep to disciples of Satan because they are not able to discern seducing, lying spirits from the Spirit of truth.

I may sound as if I am being rough on preachers, but that is because I am one. I am a pastor. I know how accountable I am for the sheep under my care. There were some older preachers who were rough on me when I was a young man trying to live for the Lord. They were blessings.

(My first sermon was titled, "You Did it Swell, But You're Going to Hell, Because You Did it *Your* Way." I began uncompromisingly telling the truth.)

On the other hand, I immediately ran into some "con men" who were evangelists and pastors. I learned the things I am writing in this chapter early in my ministry. When I started out, I thought that when God's preachers got together, there would be a time of fellowship in the Lord that would make you feel as if you had gone to the third Heaven. But I received a rude awakening.

I preached my first sermon, and afterwards, I joined some pastors in the chamber of one of the distinguished preachers in the city. I sat there a newly called preacher, waiting expectantly for words of wisdom.

And they said, "Now, that you're one of us, doc, we want to tell you something. There will be a lot of women after you. Don't let them pick you. *You* pick the one you want."

I said, "What?"

These were God's preachers who had churches and had "closed ranks" with one another. One had a girlfriend in his church and another in another church. These men circulated among conferences, slipping around drinking, smoking, cheating, lying, and misusing the church's money. They were "con men" in the pulpits. They were so charming and smooth, and they were leading people astray, lying, and misusing God's money.

It is time to begin telling the truth. God is pulling the rug out from under those kinds of preachers today. Judgment has begun at the house of the Lord. If we know God's Kingdom is being defiled, and we are not letting it be known to the people, I believe God will "get" us. However, my heart is to see Christians develop discernment enough to be able to tell who is of God and who is of the devil without being told.

Signs of Lying Spirits

If you listen carefully, you can recognize some of the things "con men" do as preachers:

• "Sisters and brothers, if you will give me $50 this Sunday, God will return you double this week."

• They may seem generous, giving back a love offering taken up for them in a church, but they know a revival is coming up at which they will really squeeze the people. They give up a little to get more. That is called "impression management."

If I impress you long enough and visit you every time you stub your toe, you will give me whatever I ask for. If I am at your beck and call all of the time, it does not matter what you hear about me, you will not believe it. I do not visit my people when they are into things they can pray for as well as I can. I go when there is real need, not to do public relations.

Of course, not everyone who returns an offering is a "con man." Some preachers genuinely hear the Spirit of truth on something like that and obey Him. Without discernment of truth, however, you will not know the difference.

• Preachers operating as "con men" may tell you the Holy Spirit is not present to empower in this age. They will tell you it is all right to fornicate, because that is what you want to hear. They will tell women to remain in abusive relationships, because the husband is the boss. (Some preachers really believe that, of course, but others say what is easiest to deal with and bring them favor with the men who usually control the pursestrings, because they really do not care about other people.)

Most people get married on their own. They did not consult God about it, and good Christian women marry thieves, crooks, and sinners. *Then* they turn it over to Jesus and expect Him to do an immediate miracle, when perhaps they were out of His will when they married. Their husbands do not want to come to Jesus, and maybe they begin to beat them every day.

Whom God sets free is free indeed. I do not believe it is God's will for women to stay in a situation where they either run the risk of being killed themselves or of doing violence to those abusive men. The best way is to let the Holy Spirit choose your spouse in the beginning, but if you find yourself in a dangerous, ungodly situation, do not hang around to be destroyed. Get out, then repent for your self-will in getting into that situation. Then *do not do it again*. Ask God first, not last.

If the unbelieving person does not want to do what is right and will not receive you, you need to allow them to leave, Paul said. (1 Cor. 7:15.) If you do not know how to distinguish what is of God and what is of the devil, you will end up giving all your affection to Satan and his things.

In John 8:44, quoted earlier in this chapter, Jesus said that Satan was not only a liar and the father of lies, but a murderer from the beginning. Do you know that if you have a lying spirit, you are murdering with your tongue? You can do more damage with that small member of the Body than most people could do with a sawed-off shotgun! (James 3:8.)

We need to get lying spirits out of the Body of Christ.

A false promise can be a lie and come from a lying spirit. If you keep promising to do something that you never do — go to church, quit drinking, stop beating your wife, take your kids somewhere — then you are operating out of a lying spirit. The ones who love you have put their futures on hold because you made a promise. They are waiting, expecting something to happen that never happens because you are lying.

Parents, if you allow your children to make idle promises they do not keep, then you are allowing a lying spirit to gain access to them. You need to deal with a child who keeps promising to bring up his grades, but does not, to see that he develops some good study habits and fulfills his promise. Otherwise, tomorrow is not going to come.

If you make promises and do not keep them, or believe promises that you know in your heart are being made in vain, then you can become so involved in a situation that you will deny anything is wrong. You become stagnant and even addicted to that situation. The only way you can exist is to come denying the truth to yourself. Then you become not only spiritually blind, but you open the door of your heart to a lying spirit on you.

The future will never come to pass if you do not deal with the present. God deals with the "right now. " He always sees everything as present tense. There is no time with God, no yesterday, today, and tomorrow. Everything is always today.

You cannot deal with your future until you get the present straight. Deal with your present. The decisions you make now *determine* your future. Do not live in the past, either. Jesus said those who put their hands "to the plough" and then look back are not fit for the Kingdom of God. (Luke 9:62.)

"Looking back" means wondering, wavering, putting off till tomorrow what you need to do today, or living in the past.

At times, I feel like a doctor doing reconstructive surgery, not on faces and bodies, but on the minds and hearts of people who have been bound in the fetters of Satan, lied to, mistreated, and abused. I feel like a doctor going in with the scalpel of the Word of God to probe the intents, desires, intellect, and hearts of people to restructure them according to the pattern of Jesus.

In addition to lying, there are other sins of the soul that will abuse and destroy you, keeping you away from God.

Two of these that are a consequence many times of living with a liar, or being under the teaching or authority of a liar, are *anger and bitterness*. The world's systems today are made up of so many lies (information and behavior that is contrary to the truth of God), that this entire younger generation seems to be full of bitterness and anger.

5

Bitterness and Anger in Christians

... And Cain was very wroth (angry), and his
countenance fell.

And the Lord said unto Cain, Why art thou wroth? and
why is thy countenance fallen?

Genesis 4:5,6

Have you ever been angry? Being angry is a natural
emotion. It is a warning mechanism. It warns us that we
are getting ready to cross over a line that we ought not to
cross. There is a kind of anger called righteous indignation
and a time and place where that is not only healthy but in
the will of God. However, righteous anger is always on the
behalf of God and His ways and at those who are
operating against His ways.

Jesus was full of righteous anger when He chased the
moneychangers and moneymakers out of the temple of
God in Jerusalem. (Matt. 21:12,13.) He was zealous on
behalf of His Father. If you see someone abusing a child or
an animal, righteous anger should rise up within you. That
person is operating against the will and principles of God.

A number of places in the Word, we can read of God's
anger and wrath against an individual or a people. But that
is God's righteousness rising up totally offended by
wickedness and unrighteousness. That is a holy anger. We
cannot get into that realm, because we are not holy. So
there is a godly anger, which we experience to a small

degree as righteous indignation, and an earthly, or fleshly, anger.

Anger that would *force* someone to accept a certain belief is not godly, because God forces no man to accept Him. He always honors the right to make choices that He gave mankind from the beginning. Even if you choose to go to Hell, God will honor that choice. It is not His will that any perish, yet He will not *make* you receive Jesus. It is your choice.

There is a certain time and place when you can cross over the line between "good" anger and "bad" anger and between anger and bitterness. If you are walking in anger, you are walking in sin. Anger will turn into wrath, and wrath manifests out of hatred. There is no love in hatred.

Jesus said, "How can you say you love God Whom you have never seen, when you don't love people you have seen?" (1 John 4:20.)

Many saints, members in good standing of the Body of Christ, carry big Bibles, wear a big cross around their neck, and sing the loudest in church. Yet they are full of anger. They have crossed the line of anger into bitterness. But they are still holding their hands up to worship God. That is a travesty of His Word.

They need to lay down their offerings, drop on their knees, and repent. (Matt. 5:23,24.) Forgiveness from God erases bitterness and counteracts anger.

Anger opens you up to a spirit of malignity, which means you wait for an opportunity to harm by word or deed that person with whom you are angry. You are waiting to "murder" that one in some way, even if it means lying about him.

There is a proverb that talks about living in a house with an angry woman:

> It is better to dwell in a corner of the housetop, than with a brawling woman in a wide house.
>
> **Proverbs 21:9**

Solomon felt so strongly about this that he repeated it in Proverbs 25:24! Brothers, if your wives are angry, get on the housetop, because you are not going to win.

Where does anger come from? Anything that is sin is not of God, so where did anger become a part of the emotions of mankind?

When you want to know something, go to the beginning of that thing in the Bible. Go to the first place that subject is talked about. That is called "the Law of the First Mention."

For anger, look at Genesis 4:5,6, quoted at the beginning of this chapter.

Anger was not an original part of man. Adam and Eve had no anger when they lived in the garden east of Eden, but anger has been part of man's nature since the fall.

Moses recorded that when Cain became very angry with Abel, his "countenance" fell. That does not mean the expression on your face, because you can look pleasant and righteous and be full of anger.

When your countenance has fallen, that means there is an attitude or a feeling about you that makes people uneasy. It is an awareness of anger and bitterness running right below the surface. You do not have to have the snarling nostrils and slavering mouth of a mad bull to be full of anger.

If the Church is going to go anywhere with God, we must learn how to love one another and not walk in anger or bitterness. We must learn to use anger as a gauge, a sign that we are moving into a dangerous place, and stop.

When you realize that your "countenance has fallen," you must also realize that you have dropped out of step with the Holy Spirit.

Anger is deceiving because it can hide in so many disguises and lead to so many other things. Someone who gets mad at the boss will get lazy on the job, hold up production, and generally mess up the flow of work.

If you are walking in anger, bitterness, or hatred, you are not walking with God, because He is love. (1 John 4:8.)

Anger can result from envy because a friend or relative gets something nice that you do not have. Then anger is apt to be expressed in criticism or backbiting of that person. Behind the facade of friendship or relationship will lurk a desire to harm that person, and hypocrisy enters into your life. You will pretend to be happy for the other person when you really wish you could destroy what they have.

In Ephesians 4:22, the apostle Paul wrote that Christians are to put off their former lifestyles (the old man) that are corrupt because of deceitful lusts.

> That ye put off concerning the former conversation (lifestyle) the old man, which is corrupt according to the deceitful lusts;
>
> And be renewed in the spirit of your mind;
>
> And that ye put on the new man, which after God is created in righteousness and true holiness.
>
> Wherefore putting away lying speak every man truth with his neighbour: for we are members one of another.
>
> Ephesians 4:22-25

Through the Holy Spirit, we have the ability to take off the fallen nature of Adam and put on the new nature that conforms to Jesus Christ. We do not have to allow anger to rise to the point of becoming bitterness that is harbored in our hearts.

Verse 23 says that we are to be *renewed* in the attitude of our minds so that we can "put on" the new man created in the pattern of the righteousness and true holiness of God. If someone does something to upset you, do not let anger and bitterness come upon you.

Anger is not justifiable when we think about what the Lord has done for us and in our lives. No matter what happens, we ourselves have committed offenses as many and as bad as those we have become so angry about.

Jesus told the men who brought a woman caught in adultery that the one among them without sin could cast the first stone at her. (John 8:7.) Therefore, anyone among us who has never sinned against anyone else might have the right to become angry and bitter. But there is no such person alive.

Walls of Bitterness

Racism begins with walls of bitterness that have been built between one people and another. Bitterness, hatred, envy, and anger all are involved in the sin of racism. If we are all one in Christ Jesus, as Paul wrote (Gal. 3:28), how can some members of the Body look down on others? The Church will never be victorious until we come to the place where all its members love one another and value one another equally, as the Lord values us.

We are the same family. We are blood relatives, no matter the color of our skin. It is the "color" of our hearts that counts in God's eyes and makes us brothers and sisters.

On the other hand, in this world, sometimes our families are the biggest sources of anger we have, or the biggest victims of our own attitudes of anger. And sometimes we have so much emotion vested in friends and relationships that we cannot deal in truth with our own families.

Paul also wrote not to let the sun go down on your anger. (Eph. 4:26.) That means, if you have an attitude toward a brother or sister, deal with it before you go to sleep. Otherwise, by morning, that anger will have turned into bitterness.

What happened prior to going to sleep will manifest in your dreams and settle as truth into your subconscious. Then you will have a much harder time getting rid of it. The situation or incident will replay over and over in your memory and become much enlarged. Then walls of bitterness will be erected between you and the other person or persons involved.

Anger will destroy you. It will shut down your capacity to love. If you are holding anger from previous relationships, you will never be able to enter wholeheartedly into a new one. Any new relationship will simply replay the problems of the previous one. How can you take anger into a fresh relationship when it should have been left behind? Do not let the sun go down on your wrath.

The Church must let go of this dirty, sinful excess baggage. Anger and bitterness are among those sins that "so easily beset us" (Heb. 12:1) and the "cares and weights" that hinder us from freely following in the footsteps of our Lord. If any local church grows, it will be only because of the love of God being manifested there.

Anger is deep-seated in some people from many times of being hurt, bruised, and afflicted. But, if it is never addressed, it will lie dormant poisoning their entire lives. Bitterness causes you to sleep all night and wake up tired, or have bouts of not being able to sleep at all. Bitterness is a force pulling on your mind and spirit. Bitterness keeps you from being able to read the Bible and pray.

How can you avoid bitterness? First of all, you can learn not to get angry, because anger is the root from which bitterness, wrath, and rage spring. The wisest man of his time, King Solomon, wrote:

He that is slow to anger is better than the mighty, and he that ruleth his spirit than he that taketh a city.

Proverbs 16:32

If you can learn to rule your own soul — mind, will, and emotions — anger will not overtake you. Being slow to get angry, Solomon said, will do you more good than being very strong. Self-control is better than being a warrior who conquers a whole city, he wrote. So one key in dealing with anger and bitterness is to be slow to anger.

Before you write a letter to someone with whom you are angry, let the ink dry on it overnight. By the time the next day rolls around, the grace of God may deal with you in a different way, and you will be very glad you did not send that letter with those hot, indignant words. So let the ink dry.

If you want to be mighty, be slow to anger. When you lose your temper, you are weak, because you are out of control. Actually, you are being controlled by the person who "pushes your button." If someone is controlling you, the devil is behind it. The person may simply be used by the devil to get a rise out of you and not purposely be coming against you. But, however it works, your real enemy is the devil. (Eph. 6:12.)

It is useless to get mad at the person. Deal with whatever it is in yourself that *can* be pushed. Then no one will be able to cause you to dance as a puppet on the strings of anger and bitterness. The devil is controlling you when you walk in anger.

Anger is a mechanism to give you warning that something is getting ready to take place, as I wrote earlier.

If anger is a warning of steam building up, why hang around for the explosion?

Suppose someone does get in your face, makes you mad, and your countenance falls. Your shoulders go back, your heart begins to beat faster, and you mouth tightens up.

• Are you going to just stand there, and let the devil push you around?

• Are you going to just let it happen when you know it is bad for your own health, and you will be miserable afterwards?

• Do you go ahead and hurt other people with your anger, sometimes even physically?

Anger and bitterness can result in heart problems and other sicknesses, if they are allowed to build up and become a way of life.

Many Christians do not deal in truth, yet we are supposed to be *about* truth. If the Body of Christ dealt with anger and bitterness, we would be a much happier people.

When you carry anger around backed up and repressed in your heart, and someone laughs, you may think they are laughing at you. Address what is being said or done instead of focusing on your feelings. Deal with situations instead of reacting to them. Then anger has no chance to get a foothold.

Proverbs 25:28 says that, if you have no self-discipline, you are like a city whose walls are broken down. In other words, you have no protection, no security. Having walls of bitterness and anger does not help. They are barriers to love going out or coming in to you. Ruling your own soul under the Holy Spirit means letting Him be your protection. That is the right kind of "wall" to have.

You can be beautiful on the outside, but all of a sudden your countenance falls, and you become ugly on the inside. Then people wonder what is going on and do not want to be around you.

Anger Is Not From God

Once you recognize that anger is a part of your character for whatever reason, begin to bring it under *your* control instead of letting it control you. Treat it as if it were a tendency to be an alcoholic. James 1:13 says that God tempts no man, so God does not send anger on you. James went on to say that every man is tempted, or drawn away from God, by his own lusts.

Some people love to be victims to the point that they will stay in a mess just for the "high" of going through arguments. There is "an adrenalin high" that comes with anger that can be like a drug. God created us with an adrenal gland that pumps spurts of extra energy into the body in times of crisis or survival. For the few minutes involved, you feel great.

Anger triggers the same substance pouring into the blood stream, and that "high" feeling can become addictive. People addicted to certain substances control that addiction by never allowing even a taste of it past their lips. You can do the same with addictive emotions. You can get so used to those feelings that you crave them and do not feel comfortable without them. Arguing and anger can be very dangerous to your health.

Godly couples do have disagreements sometimes and even get angry. However, if they truly are walking in love and under the guidance of the Holy Spirit, they will be slow to let anger loose on the other one. The Spirit will rise up within them and not let them cross the line that leads to bitterness.

There are "saved" people who are bitter toward one another because they have crossed the line of anger and even hate one another. Anger, bitterness, and hatred can become idols, things that are more important to someone than God. I wonder how long someone's salvation can remain unaffected by things like this?

Women with low self-esteem may live with ungodly men, who are committing adultery, drinking and/or gambling, and abusing them and their children. They remain in those situations sometimes because they have made gods out of the men. They think they cannot live without them.

How can those women get blessings from God? They are simply trying to use God as a crutch, something to enable them to stay with their "idols."

How can you remain in a situation as a Christian if someone is coming against everything in your life that is of God?

If you are unequally yoked with an unbeliever who is mistreating you, how can you expect God to give you financial blessings? Why? For the "heathen" to take the blessing? If you are living in the enemy's camp voluntarily, you cannot expect to pray, "Bless me, Lord," and get an answer. The answer to your situation, whatever it is, is the Holy Spirit.

Ask the Holy Spirit for wisdom, knowledge, and insight. Take time to consult Him on every aspect of your life. If you commune silently with the Holy Spirit, that will at least give you time to calm down and allow you to be slow to anger. He lives within you as an invisible guide Who will show you what to do, lead you in the right paths, and teach you how to deal with difficult situations.

All you have to do is slow down for a split second and say, "Holy Spirit, tell me what to say or do." And He will. I realize this is not "traditional" preaching to tell women in abusive situations to leave their ungodly husbands, but I believe it is Biblical. Paul said if the unsaved partner was "willing" to live with a believing wife, she should stay with him. But abusive husbands are not willing to live with *you*. They simply want victims to run over and abuse.

If Christians are going to be the Church God is looking for, we must learn how to live in this life. Trials are for your perfecting, not to make you bitter nor to endanger your life. Those are not of the will of God.

If you are in an environment where those old habits of anger and bitterness are triggered, then change your environment as well as your reactions to things. No, you cannot do it by yourself. But that is one reason we have the Holy Spirit. With His help, you can be changed more and more into the likeness of Jesus.

Why do you want to live at the same old address full of garbage and junk, when Jesus has adopted you into the family of God? You would not do that in the natural, so why do it in the Spirit? I do not live at the same old address. When you get saved, your address ought to change to "Blessed Boulevard," instead of "Going Through Avenue."

We are living in a time when preachers ought to be telling people how to live in this world, yet not be a part of it. Instead, much of the preaching going forth ignores the temptations and trials of today's society and preaches as if we still lived in the days before the Sixties' rebellion remade American society. Or preachers get in agreement with the ungodliness of our culture so that you cannot tell the difference between Christians and the unsaved.

In addition to anger and bitterness, there is another "infirmity" of the soul that causes many Christians to be dysfunctional. They love Jesus and want to serve Him, but something seems to always hold them back — and that is *shame*.

In fact, much anger and bitterness are rooted in shame.

6
The Shame That Binds

... Let us lay aside every weight, and the sin which doth
so easily beset us, and let us run with patience the
race that is set before us,

Looking unto Jesus the author and finisher of our
faith; who for the joy that was set before him endured the
cross, *despising the shame*, and is set down at the right
hand of the throne of God.

Hebrews 12:1,2

How many times have parents said, "Shame on you,"
to their children, not realizing that those words defile the
children's minds and wound their spirits? Even if your
parents did not use those words as disciplinary tools, other
words or other things that happened make a way for
shame to enter your mind.

Whether you realize it or not, there are in the deep
chambers of your subconscious mind thoughts, and
possibly, demons that torment, that tear you up every time
you want to do something for the glory of God. They are
thoughts and/or demons of shame.

Most of the demonic strongholds in your life hide in
the subconscious, where you are not aware of them unless
they manifest in your behavior and attitudes. Many times

75

other people will see shame in you, but you may not realize it is there.

Many of us walk in denial concerning shame. We do not want to admit shame is there, and the soul's defense system will cover shame with justifications or rationalizations, or you will find yourself blaming someone else for your actions.

"It's not my fault. She enticed me, and God, *You* gave her to me," Adam said, meaning, "so ultimately, *You* are to blame." (Gen. 3:12.)

If you are into lust, more than likely, you do not want to admit it. The lustful thoughts that open the door to a spirit of lust are hidden in your subconscious mind. However, that which is in your subconscious *will* eventually manifest.

You may say, "No, I have no lust. That is not me."

Yet, you *look* as if you are lusting, you *act* as if you are lusting, and you *walk* as if you are lusting. Those thoughts manifest in your attitudes and behavior, no matter how you hide them from conscious thinking.

Shame operates the same way. As babies, we are not born with shame. We are born innocent and sweet. But through toddler, preschool, adolescence, and into adulthood, many deposits of shame are made in our subconscious minds, the storage banks of our brains, the best and original "computers."

Those deposits were made by authority figures and by ourselves, as we grew aware enough of right and wrong to be ashamed of things we did or that happened to us. If we do not have proper nurturing that develops a strong sense of security and identity in us, those deposits of shame can become "toxic."

If you did not have parents or others who deposited the knowledge that you are loved no matter what you have done, you probably have large deposits of shame.

Only being brought up in the "fear and admonition" of the Lord, surrounded with a secure knowledge that His love can be trusted, protects a child from the emotions that cause him to be a dysfunctional person. Anger, bitterness, and shame will have little part in someone coming out of this kind of nurturing.

The problem is that, today, there are few homes like that. So nearly every Christian needs to deal with those three areas: anger, bitterness, and shame. Otherwise, the devil can hinder their Christian living. Demons will hinder you from going forward with God whatever way they can.

This chapter came from a message the Lord gave me specifically one Sunday. (I ask Him before every service what He wants me to tell the people.)

This time, He said, "Many of My people are suffering from toxic shame in their subconscious minds that destroys their feelings of self-worth. They are suffering because of an untrue perception of themselves."

Many Christians really don't know who they are in Christ because so much shame has built up in their lives. Instead, they try to live by emulating or imitating someone they know who does act like he, or she, "has it all together." And, of course, all of those you think are whole in their souls and spirits are really *not*. So, the only real model we should have in life is Jesus.

I had to recognize the toxic shame in my own life. The only way the Lord could impart His vision to me for ministry and our church was to heal that shame.

Shame is the excruciating internal experience of being exposed to ridicule. When someone shames you on the outside, there is an internal response. For every external, hurtful experience, something goes haywire on the inside.

Because shame is felt on the inside, not the outside, most people get pretty good at covering up shame and hurt. You can say something hurtful to someone, and they are hurt and embarrassed. Yet, in two or three seconds, they may look as if nothing happened.

You can put someone to shame by ugly words. God's people need to stop "beating up" on other people verbally. We are supposed to be God-loving and God-fearing, yet the words out of our mouths can be very nasty.

If someone you love tells you they do not love you, you might shake it off outwardly. Yet, on the inside, you are hurt and shamed. You may think you do not deserve that feeling, but you feel it anyway. Shame then can paralyze you to the point where you do not want to go on and work out the relationship.

Your subconscious will start building walls against that person.

Soon you may think, "If I keep working on this relationship, I will just get hurt again."

Shame *is* a wall that divides you from other people. If someone has shamed you, you do not want to be around that person.

If you have ever been hurt by a Christian, the shame in your subconscious may be expressed in your conscious mind by something like this:

"I'm not going to church again. All Christians are hypocrites. Those folks are phony, and I'm not going to waste my time there."

The real thought underneath the surface that you may not be aware of is:

"I am not going to expose myself again to being hurt that way. Who needs it?"

A lot of people get into shame because the devil puts condemnation on them. Condemnation breeds shame. But God said there is no condemnation to those who are in Him. (Rom. 8:1) Shame many times starts with condemnation.

Condemnation Breeds Shame

When we condemn ourselves instead of repenting and letting the blood of Jesus cover our sins, we build up large deposits of shame.

The devil knows remorse or guilt over your past is there, and he will bring that thing back to your mind over and over to get you to feel ashamed.

If you do not realize that the blood of Jesus has covered that and stop allowing the devil to bring it back up to you as if it were *not* forgiven, then whatever the sin or mistake was will haunt you the rest of your life. You will always be carrying it around as a weight on your spirit.

Instead of becoming broken (all the walls of resistance to God pulled down) and genuinely repenting so that Jesus *can* cover their pasts, many Christians try to cover their sins themselves with shame, remorse, or guilt. Shame is a counterfeit covering for the blood of Jesus. Get rid of it!

Christians are pilgrims traveling through this world, like Abraham looking for a city whose building and maker is God. (Heb. 11:10.) And as we travel, all the weights and cares of this world should be dropping off of us.

The Lord showed me that it is possible for us to divide ourselves from one another because of shame and also possible to divide ourselves from the vision He has purposed for the Body of Christ. What is God's vision for the Church?

His vision is basically the same for all churches and peoples within the Body: To have a people who serve Him as bondservants because they love Him and choose Jesus, and to use those people to fill the earth with His glory. (Num. 14:21.)

Paul wrote to the Ephesians that the ultimate purpose for the Church is this:

> To the intent that now unto the principalities and powers in heavenly places might be known by the church the manifold wisdom of God,
>
> According to the eternal purpose which he purposed in Christ Jesus our Lord.
>
> **Ephesians 3:10,11**

In order to have His family and a Kingdom on earth that will demonstrate His wisdom to the universe, the Church has to take the good news of Jesus to the entire world. God has determined to have a family made up of all peoples, tribes, languages, nations, and races. (Rev. 7:9.)

Therefore, every Christian basically has the same vision from God; however, each has a different piece of the whole. The vision for small churches is no different than that of the very largest. God's plan for how each carries out its part may be different, however.

Shame can separate you from people and things in the visible world, but also from things in the invisible world. If you are still carrying around great weights of shame, you can be blinded to God's vision for you. The devil has beguiled and tricked many of God's people to the point that they walk in shame so much they cannot do anything for God.

Most people who keep refusing the invitation to accept Jesus as Savior and Lord do so because the devil has whipped them so much over their lifestyles, habits, and behavior that they are in too much shame to respond. Somehow they feel as if they have to be clean to come to Jesus and miss the fact that they come to Him to *get* clean.

People also may be kept from coming down to the altar for salvation, deliverance, or healing because shame says, "They'll be looking at me. I'll be the focus of all eyes, and I can't do it."

Others may not speak to people about their souls for the same reason: "They may get mad at me or laugh at me."

The Lord said that if we were ashamed to own Him before men, He would be ashamed to own us before the Father. (Mark 8:38.) I have made up my mind to own Him anywhere. I do not want Him ever to say that to me.

If we, as a people, are going to catch the vision for our time, we must let go of all of the shame in us. Shame that binds also controls direction and altitude. If our attitudes are right toward God, we can move in the direction He shows us and go as high as He desires.

There is a right time for shame but it is supposed to be temporary. That is when you get in the presence of God and become convicted over your sins or over how far you are from being like Jesus. Then you need to get before the Lord with a contrite heart, one that is broken by the realization of yourself compared to His vision for you.

When you become truly repentant, shame will leave. It has served its purpose.

When you begin to grow up in the things of God, you learn how to empty yourself of shame. You were not born with it. Why carry it around with you until you die? Send the shame that binds you back to the devil and give the sin, or your feelings about things that have happened to you, to Jesus so that they will be covered by the blood.

If you truly have given something up to Jesus, you can think about it *and it will not hurt anymore.* You will no longer feel ashamed. If shame and hurt are still there, that is a good sign you are hanging onto them.

Some Christians are running around in shame and having pity parties for themselves because they missed God in some way, or because they missed the last move of God. Well, what about the second go-round? Get up out of shame, and do not make the same mistake the next time. God is a just God, quick to forgive us if we repent. (1 John 1:9.)

Perhaps you say, "But I have committed the same sin over and over."

Jesus has not come yet, so things are not over. Get up and try again! We let the devil knock us down and put us in shame, then we wallow in it as if we could not get up. That is a falsehood. The devil is weighing you down so you will think you cannot get up out of the mud and repent. The Lord, on the other hand, is tarrying for you to get up.

Toxic Shame Must Be Eliminated

We must get the toxic shame out of the Church. When you become "intoxicated," you are in a state that is not good for you and full of a substance that is harmful. That substance has permeated your bloodstream and your brain. Your thought processes are affected. Your eyesight and hearing are affected, as well as your balance.

The Church must get rid of the shame that has so intoxicated us as to make us dysfunctional. We are not able to "walk the chalk line" God has marked out before us. As long as we are dealing with shame, we are not really going anywhere with God.

Every time you want to ride high with the Lord, the devil knows what string to pull that will trigger the shame in your subconscious mind that you are denying.

The Lord has anointed my wife and me to minister in this area. He has given me more insight about women and my wife about men. I have noticed that the first thing a woman does to fight shame is change her hair in some way. (Now that does not mean every woman who changes her hair is in shame!) They do that because they are trying to find a new look. The old look is associated in their minds with something that shamed them.

My wife says that when men are dealing in shame they tend to pretend nothing is the matter. Nothing is going wrong, and they have total control of their situations, they say. They do not need anyone's help, because they know what they are doing.

Instead of saying, "Man, I missed it," or "I'm hurt. You hurt my feelings," they act macho and cover up with a strong shield of masculinity.

A man needs respect, and a woman needs affection. If she does not get the affection she needs, she will not give him any respect. Take a look at Genesis 3:8-13, when Adam and Eve faced God after their disobedience.

> **And they heard the voice of the Lord God walking in the garden in the cool of the day: and Adam and his wife hid themselves from the presence of the Lord God amongst the trees of the garden.**

> And the Lord God called unto Adam, and said unto him, Where art thou?
>
> And he said, I heard thy voice in the garden, and I was afraid, because I was naked; and I hid myself.
>
> And he said, Who told thee that thou wast naked? Hast thou eaten of the tree, whereof I commanded thee that thou shouldest not eat?
>
> And the man said, The woman whom thou gavest to be with me, she gave me of the tree, and I did eat.
>
> And the Lord God said unto the woman, What is this that thou hast done? And the woman said, The serpent beguiled me, and I did eat.

If you notice, the man got into shame before the woman. Although she actually first ate the fruit, he knew that he was accountable. Men can be blessings or curses to women. A bad man will keep a woman down, into shame, and dragging the ground. Many men are "intoxicated" with shame, and they dump the "toxic waste" onto their wives.

We find three things that began to open up when man first sinned:

1. Shame;

2. Fear;

3. Blame of others.

Adam first became ashamed and made something with which to cover Eve and himself. Then he became fearful and tried to hide from God. The third thing he did was to *accuse* Eve and, indirectly, God. God does not shame us, nor does He give us a spirit of fear. (2 Tim. 1:7.) And He certainly does not want us to blame other people for our own sins or problems.

In Exodus 32 is the story of how Israel staged a huge orgy worshipping an idol while Moses was up on Mt. Sinai getting the laws of God for them. The Lord told Moses to get down the mountain, because the people had corrupted themselves. (Ex. 32:7.)

In Exodus 32:25, Moses saw that the people were naked, and the verse says: **for Aaron had made them naked unto their shame among their enemies.** Then Moses called for everyone on the Lord's side to move over next to him, and all the sons of Levi (the tribe from which Moses and Aaron came) moved over to him.

That is how the Levites became the royal priesthood. They were loyal to God. If you are loyal to God, you will not be in shame. Then the loyalty of the Levites was immediately tested. The Lord told them to get a sword and kill those who participated in the idol worship. (v. 27.) The Bible says some three thousand men were slain that day.

When Adam and Eve ate the fruit, they chose the visible, natural world. With that came vanity, sensual pleasure, and worldly wisdom, which means trying to figure everything out with the mind rather than trusting God and simply obeying.

When you choose the visible, you set yourself up for the punishment, the consequences, of the visible. Adam and Eve set all mankind up for this, but we have personal choices that determine how much of those natural consequences fall on us individually. God's forgiveness does not always eliminate the consequences.

If you have been out in the world living a perverted lifestyle or simply indulging in fornication or adultery, you can come to God and repent and have those sins totally washed away as if they had never happened. *However,* if you have contracted some communicable disease such as AIDS, the "wages" of that sin may ruin, or even take, your life.

Many patients have died with AIDS (contracted from sexual sin) who are going to Heaven, because they went to God broken and repentant for sinning against Him. But they suffered on earth, because in the beginning, they chose the visible things that seemed to offer pleasure.

If you are walking with your eyes focused on the visible, you are walking in one of these three: lust of the flesh, lust of the eyes, or pride of life. The sins that are included in those three categories control you, because you have chosen to become "hooked up" with them. You have voluntarily placed yourself in bondage to Satan.

How To Get Rid of Shame

A victorious Christian must get to the point of walking through the visible world to get to the invisible. Simply because you are having bad thoughts does not mean you are controlled by the Lord, however. You can cast down those vain imaginations. (2 Cor. 10:5.)

God has called Christians to be His royal priesthood in their generations (1 Pet. 2:9), but we cannot move out under the priestly anointing as long as we are in shame. The priestly anointing is a ministry of intercession, of reconciling people to God. How can you win someone to Christ, when you are living in toxic shame?

How can you be responsible to birth someone into the Kingdom when you are just hanging on by the "hair of your chinny-chin-chin" yourself? Your prayer life is sporadic, because every time you begin to pray, the devil is there shaming you.

I am tired of hearing people say, "I'm so unworthy to pray, so unworthy to read the Bible, so unworthy to minister."

In the flesh and before we come to Jesus, *everyone* is unworthy. However, after you are saved, His blood has *made* you worthy. When you say you are unworthy after you have been washed in the blood of Jesus, you are offending against the blood. You are saying Jesus' sacrifice on Calvary was not enough to cover you.

God does not war against you. Satan wars against you, and *you* end up warring against God. However, if you will surrender your will to Him, and let Him cleanse you totally, you can do what His will is for you. You can fulfill His plan and purpose in your life.

The bottom line is that shame is sin, just as fear is sin. Guilt and condemnation, anger and bitterness, and all of the other lusts of the flesh and eyes are sin, as well as the pride of life. Everything that is not of God is sin, and grace does not cover unrepented sin.

You must get your sins under the covering of the blood of Jesus, so that you can walk under the protection of God's grace. Once you give something to the Lord and leave it there, the power of God will keep it subdued. Then you will have no more bondage to your old nature or old situations, and the devil cannot pull on you.

A Christian needs to constantly evaluate himself and repent of everything that is not of God. If you judge yourself, Jesus said, you will not have to be judged. (Matt. 7:1,2.) He did not mean that in the sense of those who hold themselves to impossible standards of perfection and condemn themselves. *Judging* means evaluating, checking your attitudes and behavior against those you know are like Jesus, then repenting of the ones that are not.

Once you repent, *let* go of them. If you still are weighed down by your shortcomings after you have prayed and repented, then you are dealing with shame and not receiving forgiveness. Go back and repent of the shame, repent of trying to punish yourself, and let the Holy Spirit cleanse the shame and guilt off of your soul.

Once you get a revelation of how shame feels and the fact that it is different from conviction, all it takes is one good time on your face before the Lord. You can give up everything to Him and get up with your slate clean. The words of Jesus to sinners always were, "Go and sin no more." He never condemned them nor shamed them.

First John 2:15 says not to love the world nor the things that are in the world. Those who love the world, John said, do not have the love of God in them. That is pretty straightforward and blunt! If you are subject to what you see, and what you see is controlling you, you are tied to the world.

Shame is nothing but a vain thing. Cast it down, and when you have cast down shame, you can truly see the eternal blessedness and hope of what God has done through Jesus. You can appropriate what He has done for yourself. When you do that, you dislodge toxic shame from the past, because you truly have a revelation that you are a new person. You can fully understand that the person you used to be and the things you used to do no longer have any control over you.

Paul wrote along this line to the Christians at Ephesus:

> And you hath he quickened, who were dead in trespasses and sins;
>
> Wherein in time past ye walked according to the course of this world, according to the prince of the power of the air, the spirit that now worketh in the children of disobedience:
>
> Among whom also we all had our conversation (manner of living) in times past in the lusts of our flesh, fulfilling the desires of the flesh and of the mind; and were by nature the children of wrath, even as others.
>
> But God, who is rich in mercy, for his great love wherewith he loved us,

Even when we were dead in sins, hath quickened us together with Christ, (by grace ye are saved;)

And hath raised us up together, and made us sit together in heavenly places in Christ Jesus:

That in the ages to come he might shew the exceeding riches of his grace in his kindness toward us through Christ Jesus.

Ephesians 2:1-7

That tells us that everyone has a bad track record. The Body of Christ has former alcoholics, junkies, whoremongers, and even murderers in it. But once they are raised up from the dead state of their sins, they sit in heavenly places with Jesus as much as the person who never committed any carnal sins.

Those who never sinned, according to our ideas of sin, are just as guilty in God's eyes. Man's righteousness, no matter how "good," is as filthy rags in the sight of God. (Isa. 64:6.) Only what He does through us and in us is truly good.

Paul was saying, "At one time, the world controlled you, but the world has no more hold on you now, because you do not walk in shame."

As long as you stay in denial about the things that are in your mind — anger, bitterness, fear, or shame — you will not see the face of God, because you will not be broken enough to see the things of the invisible. The visible is the temporal (the temporary) and the invisible is the eternal.

Shame keeps you from getting in one accord with the people of God, and the Holy Spirit cannot manifest in His fullness until God's people in a place are in one accord. (Acts 2:1,5:12.) The fire of the Holy Spirit manifested as tongues of fire in Jerusalem on the Day of Pentecost. Fire is a form of sanctification and purification, and the Holy Spirit comes as a wind of judgment.

When people get real with God and become filled with the Holy Spirit, they need to know God has already judged them, placed their sins on the altar of sacrifice, and the fire of God has consumed them. When you have truly been with the Holy Spirit, you are never the same.

If you are walking in darkness, gloom, and shame, judgment has not yet come to your house. The fire of Pentecost has not yet sanctified you. A lot of people are going around playing at speaking in tongues. But I want to tell you real tongues are fluent and complete, not just syllables repeated over and over.

The present-day Church is dysfunctional because it is operating in the temporal realm: presenting activities, offering gimmicks to get people to come in, having raffles, and so forth. The Church today, in the majority, is not about getting people saved and filled with the Holy Spirit so they can live in the eternal realm.

The Church is too full of hidden agendas.

7

Apples Do Not Fall Too Far From the Tree

And thou shalt love the Lord thy God with all thine heart, and with all thy soul, and with all thy might.

[Jesus added, Thou shalt love thy neighbour as thyself — Matt. 22:39.]

And these words, which I command thee this day, shall be in thine heart:

And thou shalt teach them diligently unto thy children ....

Deuteronomy 6:5-7

The more we look at the dysfunctions in the Christian life, the more we can see there are things in people's pasts that slow their progress in the things of God. Many Christians hear the truth with their natural ears but not with their spiritual ears. Then the truth of God's Word becomes like water running off a duck's back. It hits and falls right off.

God told Eve that her descendants would bruise the head of the serpent. (Gen. 3:15.)

When Isaac and Rebecca had twins, Jacob came out holding Esau by the heel. That is why he was named *Jacob*, which means "trickster." (Gen. 25:26.) And that is what Satan does. He can trick you out of your inheritance, but that is all he can do. *You can bruise his head.*

91

He "grabs hold of your heel" by replaying your past before you. He triggers feelings of inadequacy in you and makes you feel cheap, tarnished, tired, and worn. He tries to keep you under a yoke of bondage, and the "yoke" is *fear.* So many people walk in fear, and if you walk in fear, you cannot have faith.

God said that it was impossible to please Him without faith. (Heb. 11:6.) If you walk in fear, then you do not truly love the Lord. Paul wrote that *perfect love* casts out fear. (1 John 4:18.)

Jesus said, "If you are not keeping My commandments, you do not really love Me." (John 14:15.)

If you cannot walk out of anger, bitterness, and shame, then the devil has a stronghold somewhere in you that has not been dealt with. Some scenario, some incident or event in your past is still as fresh in your subconscious as if it were in the present, as if it had just happened. It is still influencing your life.

If you were abused by a parent or another close relative, and that has not been rectified through forgiveness and healing, then that incident is engrafted in your foundational mind. That scenario is still running in your mind. All the devil has to do is press the right button and your computer-brain will bring the images up to your conscious mind to remind you of all of the horrible things you lived through.

Also, if you were abused, and that hurt is not dealt with, chances are very good that you will become an abuser of your own children. It is a fact that "apples do not fall too far from the tree."

Take one woman who had high expectations for her daughter. However, in her own life, she had been the loosest woman you ever want to run into. She was in the clubs, having parties, bringing men in the side door when she thought her baby girl was asleep. But the baby was not asleep.

Then the baby grew up, and Mama was saying, "Girl, don't you run around with So-and-so. He's no good. Don't get pregnant and bring a baby here for me to bring up. I'll put you out of the house."

While she was talking, something clicked in her mind, and she remembered her own mother saying things like that.

She remembered her mother saying, "I don't care what you see me do. Don't do what I do; do what I say."

History repeats itself generation after generation. That sounds rough, but it is true. If the father was an alcoholic or the mother is an abuser, chances are the son and daughter will be the same. Or possibly the daughter abused by the father will marry a man who carries on the abuse.

Perhaps it is not parental abuse but a bad relationship in the past. If that thing was never rectified so that the hurt is still there, you need some help. And these things cannot be dealt with alone. Where does your help come from? It comes from above.

Take a father who expects a lot of his son. He loves the son, but somehow, he expects him to be everything he was and more. If he always wanted to be a great athlete, many times he will project that identity off on the son. Or if he *was* a good athlete, he may expect the son to be one, when in reality, the son has no abilities or desires in that direction.

This kind of situation can set up rejection, shame, guilt, and other strongholds in a child's mind.

The son is just six years old, say, and the apple of his father's eye. But the strong and brawny father is unrealistic about things. He throws a ball up into the air and says, "Catch it, son!"

There the boy is in a hat bigger than his head, wearing a glove bigger than both hands, looking way up into the sky at something coming at him. He is thinking he cannot catch the ball before it even gets close to him. The task looks gigantic to him.

He thinks, "If I don't catch it, Daddy is going to get mad at me. If I miss the ball, I'm going to let him down."

And Daddy is saying, "Be my little man and make me proud of you."

So the boy gets ready, "It's coming, Daddy. I don't see it, but it is coming down. Look at me, Daddy! See how I look? Don't I look good, Daddy?"

And the ball comes down, kerplunk, on the ground and not in the little boy's glove.

If the father has any love of God and any real love of the boy, he will say, "That's okay. We'll just keep practicing, and I'll show you how," or "It took me a long time to learn how to do this, too."

He will reaffirm that he loves the boy whether he is good at playing ball or not.

But suppose the father says, "I thought you were my little man, and you can't even catch a ball. I'm through with you, boy. You can't catch. You can't run. You can't do anything. Go play with your sister's dolls."

That man has made a great deposit of shame in his child. He has sinned against the child's mind, so that a stronghold has been opened up through hurt. The enemy now has a place to get a foothold in that child.

Harvest Comes From What Is Sown

God's law says that what is sown will be reaped. We

think of that as getting back what you give out. However, it is true of any "crop." If you sow hurt and rejection into a child's mind, the harvest in that child's adult life will be hurt and rejection. If shame is sown, shame is what runs an adult's life.

If you sow the love of God in a child's Life, when he is old he will not depart from God. (Prov. 22:6.)

Black people have scenarios in their minds that come from being taught they are supposed to be poor, that being black is not only wrong but bad. We have strongholds of inferiority.

I did not realize that I was intelligent until I was in junior high school. I had the idea that blacks are not intelligent instilled in me. Unless your parents instilled in you that you could achieve, that you were somebody, you will very likely not be a success in life.

Something clicked in me when I found out intelligence is not just a characteristic of white people. So I began to push forward and make efforts to achieve in life. I found that I could do all things through Christ Who strengthened me. (Phil. 4:13.) I got that from the Bible, not from the people around me as I grew up.

I have many hurting people in my church, who are suffering from a lack of nurturing and from scenarios in their pasts that hinder them from being functional Christians. God has assigned me to teach them how to go back into the memories of their pasts and disarm all of the little devices, buttons, and strings Satan wants to pull to keep them from following the will of God.

Until Jesus came, there was no way for man to be reconciled to God, because man was "brain damaged." Without the way that Jesus made for us, we cannot think right or act right. We are always in chaos, confusion, and messes. Your mind is messed up until it is made to conform to Jesus.

I was "brain damaged" until I became born again. So were you. All of us have things from the past in us that will continually come up if they are not dealt with. They are damaged areas of our minds.

The thing we have to do is ask a "super psychiatrist," Jesus, to show us the things that have hurt us, blinded or wounded us, and shamed us. Then we have to ask the Holy Spirit to clean all of those negative emotions out of us and heal the wounds of the past.

I could not teach this or write about it if I had not experienced it for myself. My wife and I sat up until way in the night once, talking and writing, writing and talking, as we asked the Lord to show us scenarios from our pasts that needed to be dealt with. And, just as you will find in your own experience, there were some things He showed us that we did not want to see!

However, the truth set us free, and it will set you free. You not only have a will, but God gave you the right to use it. You can choose to be set free or continue to walk bound by things of the past. If you are serious about becoming functional in the will of the Lord, seek to find your dysfunctions in the Holy Spirit until you are set free.

Turn the phone off, so that people cannot call you and dump garbage into your spirit. Lock yourself in with the Lord, and do not come out until He has cleansed and blessed you.

Get down on your knees and say, "Lord, I need some answers, and I'm not getting up from here until you satisfy me."

I can personally tell you this works, because once I locked myself in with God for a week. I had to have an answer. I was going out of my mind, hurt on the inside so badly that I kept backsliding and moving away from God. Until I got an answer to what was destroying me on the inside, I stayed on my face. No bread and no water passed my lips until my prayers were answered.

People may say you are not anything, that you are not going to make it. You may have been told all your life that you will never amount to anything. But God says His grace is sufficient. He says He will deal with your past until it is dead, and you are "raised" from the dead a new person.

Your mind is like a movie camera that takes pictures and records events in your life, and if those events have not been dealt with, they are still there.

Your soul has those things on film, and the film must be erased by the power and might of God. Otherwise, you will either replay those things and be pulled into them again or you will walk in self-condemnation.

Every time you begin to do something powerful for God, the devil will trigger a replay of that event in your mind. The next thing you know, you have moved away from the presence of the Holy Spirit and there is no anointing of power. The presence of the Holy Spirit for His works, which we call "the anointing," will break the yoke of bondage. (Luke 4:18.)

God Wants To Make Over Your Personality

Everyone has a temperament and a character. Those two things come together to make up a person's personality. Your character, or your nature, the kind of person you really are, is manifested through your temperament. Your character is formed by your upbringing, by the kind of nurturers you had, whether they were your parents or other people who looked after you.

Some people have bad characters, and some have good. If you had the kind of nurturing where you saw people flying off the handle at one another, backbiting and gossiping, or lying and cheating, then that is in your character whether you like it or not, whether you admit it or not. It is part of your makeup.

You may be manifesting a good temperament now, but when the right button is pushed, you will go off just as your nurturers did. That is why experts say a child who is abused usually will grow up to become an abuser. That is why people say they have to manifest a temper because their father, grandfather, uncles, and so forth did. It "runs in the family."

But it does not have to run over *you*.

God wants to make over your personality. He wants to help you conform to the image of Christ, not the image of Daddy or Grandpa, and certainly not the image of the devil, "father" of the fallen nature. You do not have to be a victim of your past. You can change your environment. Today, however, we do not have a lot of preaching along the line of sanctification, helping people let go of themselves and conform to the image of Jesus.

Too many churches have hidden agendas that get in the way of preaching the simple story of Jesus and Him crucified and our command to be like Him, to love God with our whole hearts and our neighbors as ourselves. (Matt. 22:37-39.)

Too many pastors have hidden agendas that get in the way of their simply being obedient to carry out God's agenda for them and their congregations. Hidden ambition gets in the way of teaching people how to live sanctified lives dedicated to the ways of God.

Too many Christians cannot be bothered to follow God's agenda in their lives, causing them to be conformed to the image of Jesus. Instead, their agendas are to get God to do something for them in the area of financial prosperity, getting them husbands or wives, better jobs, or whatever.

8
Hidden Agendas in the Church

*... The harvest truly is great, but the labourers are few:
pray ye therefore the Lord of the harvest, that he would
send forth labourers into his harvest.*

Luke 10:2

The fields are white and ripe for harvest, and God's agenda for the Body of Christ is found in the Great Commission (Mark 16:15-18): Go into all the world and preach the Gospel, casting out demons, and healing the sick. Signs and wonders will follow those who do this, Jesus said.

Why do we see so few signs and wonders today? It is because too few of us are following God's agenda. We have our own agendas that are hidden from plain sight. Our agendas are not immediately visible and sometimes are covered over with a pretense of carrying out God's plan for us.

If you have one agenda over here, and I have another over there, how are we going to get together to perfect the saints for the work of the ministry (Eph. 4:12), much less to get organized enough to go harvest the "wheat"? Personal agendas are one big reason that the Church today is dysfunctional.

Each denomination and most local churches have their own agendas, and not very many of them involve lost souls. Every time a church splits, it is because someone had a hidden agenda. You cannot go forth as an "independent" from the Body without deviating from God's agenda.

When God is ready for you to go out, He will send you from a local body as part of it. We have people in our church who want to go out and "fight the devil."

I say, "Well, you need a covering to go fight the devil, people to love you and pray for you."

But sometimes the person will say, "No, I am going to be independent."

What can I do but let him go? Then he is out there without a covering, with no intercessors, getting beat up, buffeted, and kicked by the enemy. He had a hidden agenda and walked away from the covering God put him under.

If you say God sent you to a certain church, you should stay there until He moves you. Learn to be a servant in that place. Find out what God's agenda is for it and fall in line. Do not develop your own agenda.

I have seen men move into a church saying God sent them there and then, when they thought they were powerful enough and had enough support (like Absalom, 2 Sam. 15), they took the cloak off their hidden agendas that became "monsters," not God-birthed spiritual children. Those agendas clashed with the one God had given the man sent to that place in the beginning, of course.

A man or a woman with a hidden agenda influences little baby lambs to follow them, and what happens is that then the "lambs" are out of line, out of position, and not in a place to receive from God. Anyone who is ambitious for natural things is not going to make it with God.

An ambitious person will do everything he can to propagate his own plans and his own advancement. He will step on people to get where he wants to go and maneuver behind the scenes to find favor with pastors so he will be allowed in their pulpits.

I know what this is like, because I have been there. When I first started in the ministry, I had my own agenda. I had things all worked out to build a big ministry. I made friends with other preachers who had churches, and I knew the location of every church in the whole country with a vacant pulpit.

There is a newsletter that lists churches with no pastors. Whenever a church has a vacant pulpit, they send notices to this paper. A minister actually can preach all year visiting churches that do not have pastors. You can go several places in every state.

I liked North Carolina, so I sent a resume to churches in the Raleigh/Durham area, and others to Rome, Georgia. But I was building my own agenda. That is not the way to "build" a ministry. Ask God to put you in a place where you can be under the kind of leadership He wants, leadership that will develop you to the point where you can fit into His agenda.

Then ask God to give you wisdom, strength, and humility enough to help that man or woman fulfill God's agenda for *them*. In God's scheme of things, you must learn to be a servant before He can make you into His kind of leader. Your ministry will unfold while you are learning to serve.

The church I pastor today, Greater Mt. Zion, is not my thing. It does not belong to me. I have no hidden agenda and could walk out tomorrow if God said to go. My job is not to make a name and reputation for myself, but to try my best to move God's vision for this church forward to where He wants it to be.

Just because God puts you into a pulpit does not mean that you walk a little bit higher than other people or that you cannot sweep sidewalks or wash windows anymore. Once you are a pastor, you are supposed to be doing *more* service than before.

Many young preachers develop their hidden agendas because they only see the pastors being "front and center" during services. But pastoring is a 24-hour-a-day warfare with the devil. Pastoring God's way is not a picnic or a way to be personally glorified.

Young people have hidden agendas from their parents. The parents' agenda is for their children to be well-educated, to become established in life, and then to find the "right" spouse. Christian parents have an open agenda with the top priority being for their children to develop good relationships with God.

Parents' agendas usually are:

• "While you are in my house, you are going to do what I say."

• "You have to be home at a certain time."

• "Do not talk back to me."

• And, to girls, "You will not have some boy here while I'm at work or not home."

However, many times, boys or girls operate on a hidden agenda of being popular with the opposite sex. They get on the phone when parents are not home, pass letters in school, and eat lunches together. Their agendas run counter to their parents and, oftentimes, following those hidden agendas brings them more trouble than they can walk out the rest of their lives.

God's Agenda Is the Only One That Works

God gives His agenda, His vision, to the leader of a church, who is to expose it to the congregation as the Lord wills. However, a wise pastor will watch for those coming into his church who may have hidden agendas. For example, the zeal of the new-born or newly called Christian sometimes can be his own downfall and cause a lot of trouble in a church.

Usually, new Christians think of themselves as more spiritual and more mature than they are. They are full of zeal without knowledge. They came in confused, raggedy, beat up by the devil, sin-sick, and full of rebellion. Then they get saved and turn all of the ambition and other old-nature attitudes into building a place in the church. Many times they immediately develop hidden agendas, whose success is based on the dog-eat-dog, step-on-other-people-to-get-ahead tactics of the world.

I get phone calls like this one fairly often:

"Good morning, Pastor! God has shown me that I am supposed to preach for you. I am really drawn to your ministry."

I thought, "Well, it is kind of unusual that God did not tell me about *you*," but I said, "I'm sorry, but I am leaving for an out-of-town meeting. Call me back."

I have not heard from that preacher since. He was testing the water to see if there was room to slide his hidden agenda into services in our church.

Another way hidden agendas manifest is with people who volunteer to serve in the church, but want to pick where they serve and what they do. As leader, the pastor should have enough spiritual insight to know where to place those who volunteer.

Your "gift" (calling) will make room for you. If you truly are called and honestly want to serve God, do not go around knocking on doors. Wait for God to open them.

How can you be ordained by God to serve in a certain place and go contrary to the one He has set in charge there?

If God wants you to be a famous evangelist, that will come to pass — if you do not mess it up by going off and doing your own thing. When you have a hidden agenda, destruction is your end. You better bury that thing before it buries you.

When King Saul saw that he had lost a strategic battle and the curse the prophet Samuel had pronounced over him years before was about to come to pass, he asked his armourbearer to kill him before the enemy did. The armourbearer did not have the vision of his leader. He refused, so Saul leaned on his own sword and died. (1 Sam. 31:4.) Then the armourbearer "leaned" on his own sword and died. (1 Sam. 31:5.)

However, a young Amalekite came upon the death scene, and he had a hidden agenda. He thought he could find favor with the new king, David, by pretending to have killed Saul, thereby doing David a favor. But David knew God's will and heart said, "Touch not My anointed ones and do my prophets no harm" (I Chron. 16:22; Ps. 105:15), so the armourbearer found his own destruction instead of fame and fortune. David killed him the way he had pretended to kill Saul. (2 Sam. 1:1-16.)

It is easy for a spirit of ambition to take root in your mind, and if it does, it will sidetrack you from where you are supposed to be. Ambition and selfishness run hand in hand. To follow God's agenda, you must not have one of your own, and you must learn to follow orders. What good would it do God to have five Elijahs in any church and no Elishas?

God's agenda is not for the choir to make albums, or for a church to have a school. But, if that church is doing the work of the ministry according to God's plan, those things may happen. The key is to have your eyes on God, not on various aspects of ministry.

If you know how to serve, your reward will be great. God will give you greater things to do. But if you do not know how to serve, being a pastor is not easy for you. When you learn to serve, pride disappears. You forget about what people think and how you look.

Pride must die for God to really be able to use you in great ways. Anyone with carnal ways — pride, anger, bitterness, or sins of the flesh — is of limited good to God, and sooner or later, He will expose the sin in that person's life. God does not look at your ambition and desires. Neither does He look at your abilities or talents. He looks at the attitude of your heart.

I believe God is pulling the cloak off hidden agendas today, so that His people will be able to see clearer than ever who is truly serving God and doing His will in His way and His time.

There are other people who have "hidden" agendas far different from those fueled by ambition. These people have agendas of living "ordinary" lives, of being plain, pew-sitting Christians, when God's plan for them is to move out in ministry. These are the ones who run from God's call on their lives.

I also was one of those. I ran from the call to preach for an entire year, but the calling became so heavy on me that I could not function. I thought I was going crazy. It was not until I surrendered to God that I was again able to see right, walk right, and talk right.

Sometimes teachers fight callings, but what if you are the only teacher to whom some people will be receptive? If you refuse to teach, think of all the people who will not get ministered to because you refused. Think of all those who may be lost forever because your agenda was not the one God had for you.

If I had known this principle earlier, I would have done a whole lot of things differently. If I had known that money will follow you if you do what pleases God, I would have made some different decisions. You may be struggling to get into business. Well, everything will fall into place when you give your all to Jesus.

If you are having financial problems, get it all together with God. Do what God said to do in His principles. Money problems can stem from not having enough and also from not knowing what to do with what you have.

People get the attitude, "I'm not going to work hard or do this or that to make *him* look good," (talking about the pastor).

Serving in a church to help God's vision for that place be fulfilled is not making a man or woman look good. It is making God look good. Whatever you do should be done for the glory of God. Some people just do enough to be able to say they work in the church.

The local church is the only place I know of that you can come, lounge around, get fed, and do nothing or give nothing. Church usually is a place where everyone will smile at you but not deal with you the way you ought to be dealt with.

Attitudes Need Constant Checking

All of us ought to periodically check ourselves for attitudes of the heart and attitudes toward service. If you have been slothful, you should get off your "do-nothing" and find something to do in your local church. But ask the leaders what they need you to do. Do not go in there setting your own agenda and choosing what you will and will not do. If you have something to offer, offer it, but be willing and happy to do whatever needs doing.

One of the biggest attitudes that hinders Christians is rebellion against authority. In this country, we cannot follow leadership. Each American thinks he is the final authority on everything. This stems from the attitude of independence that has been here since the Revolutionary War and from the emphasis on self that has been an integral part of our society since the Sixties.

The "Me Generation" is in the Church, as well as in secular society, and has contributed to the dysfunctional state of the Body of Christ. How can you serve if you will not follow the leader set over you? Spirits of Absalom and Jezebel easily find places in most of our churches and ministries because Christians are full of rebellion.

The nation of Islam is an example of the other extreme. They do not ask questions; they just do what they are told. They carry obedience to the point of being a fault, of course. However, there *is* a happy medium. Christians are to obey those set over them (Heb. 13:17) as long as their instructions do not conflict with God's.

The Church is divided against itself, so how can we go into corporate warfare and win? If all of the churches in an area would give up their hidden agendas, and if all of the preachers would do likewise, could we not do a greater job? If all Christians in a town or city were following the same agenda — God's — couldn't they accomplish what He wills? Of course they could.

I am for the Body of Christ coming together with the same agenda. Even if I were not the one named pastor of a city-wide group, I would support it if I knew God had done it. I would take a back seat and serve wherever God told me was my place.

God gives the vision for a place to the leader He has called there, and the leader exposes that vision to the people. If the pastor is truly following God, the people in that place need to fall in line behind him. Not accepting a pastor as one sent from God to them has been the downfall of many a church or group.

But some people do not want to serve. They do not "feel" like working. Let me tell you, serving God is not based on how you feel. Many Sunday mornings, I may not feel like getting out of bed, preparing a message, and standing in front of a group of people being responsible for what they receive that day.

I know, however, that if I stay in bed, I not only will be a disobedient servant, but slothfulness will zap my strength. I will end up feeling worse than if I got up. When it came time for me to do what God had for me to do, I would be tired, listless, and no use to Him.

So, again, let me assure you that what Christ has for you to do is not based on what you feel, nor on what you think you should be doing. You may not *feel* like doing what the pastor or the elders ask you to do in the ministry of helps, but do it anyway as unto the Lord.

Again, have some common sense: If someone tells you to do something that is going to affect your health, break up your marriage, or cause you to sin, that is not of God, and you are not bound to do that thing. But if you are asked to so something pertaining to the things of God, you ought to do it quickly and as best you can.

Those who are faithful over the little things are the ones who are given more to do. (Matt. 25:21.)

You can tell if you are living in submission and obedience by the warfare that comes against you. Have you ever had to defend your Christianity? If you are not living it, you will not have to defend it. If you are not having something or someone put pressure on your ability to stand, then you are living too comfortably to be a working vessel for the Lord.

I do not preach "sugar water" nor give my people a lot of "candy" messages. The teachers and preachers sent us by God are teachers of truth and not of error. They are preachers of righteousness, and I delegate authority to them, expecting the congregation to listen to them as if it were me.

Also, I ask the Lord to shake up my church.

I say, "Lord, if you see any branch in my church that is not producing, water it a little longer, Lord. But if it does not produce fruit, cut if off. That branch is sapping strength from the tree. It is taking in food and water, but not producing."

Older Christians should never "retire" and sit at home watching soap operas or other trash, as I wrote in an earlier chapter. God has no retirement plan. The minute someone does this, his body thinks it is finished with life and begins to take on infirmities. The devil will come and load people up with sicknesses, if they remain idle in the Lord's Kingdom.

I met a 64-year-old preacher not long ago who could throw weights around like a young man. He loved the Lord, and he has stayed active. So he is able to still carry a load for God as he ages. Do not think you are too old to do anything for God. The more you do for God, the better you will feel. The reason you get stiff is that you are not doing anything.

Get out of that easy chair. Go out on the street and pass out tracts. Lift your hands and do spiritual aerobics praising the Lord.

All of the things I have written about, of course, depend on a person's truly having been born again. Some dysfunctional Christians are that way because they *think* they are born again when they are not. If you have never been born again, or if you are not sure about your salvation, please read the last chapter of this book very carefully.

Being "born again" makes you a new creature, a member of a new race born of "the last Adam" and "the Second Man," Jesus.

And so it is written, The first man Adam was made a living soul; the last Adam was made a quickening spirit.

1 Corinthians 15:45

The truly functional Church consists totally of blood-bought and blood-washed children of God.

9
The Necessity of Being Born Again

Jesus answered and said unto him (Nicodemus), Verily, verily, I say unto thee, Except a man be born again, he cannot see the kingdom of God.

. . . Except a man be born of water and of the Spirit, he cannot enter into the kingdom of God.

That which is born of the flesh is flesh; and that which is born of the Spirit is spirit.

Marvel not that I said unto thee, Ye must be born again.

John 3:3,5-7

We are living in a time when society is trying to dictate the agenda of God's Church. We are getting to the point where government wants to legislate what a preacher preaches, where he can go, and what he can do. Street preachers are being locked up for disturbing the peace. There is very little respect today for God's people.

If this is so, and we can see that it is, there must be an internal crisis, a war, going on for total control of society. Satan is the prince of power of this world *and* of the air. (John 12:31; Eph. 2:2.) He controls television, radio, and just about all of the media and entertainment businesses. Many churches cannot afford air time.

However, I believe there is coming a time when those barriers will come down, and the message of God will go

113

forth unfettered. But if you are tied up in the visible world, you cannot understand the things of God, no matter how much they are preached and taught.

I believe that, to be functional, we need to back up and look at the very first step in building the Church. God must have a people who are truly and genuinely born again. Jesus said His Church would be built on the rock of belief that He, truly all man, was just as truly the Son of God. (Matt. 16:18.)

Jesus told Nicodemus that he *must* be born again, which means that every person who wants to have eternal life with God also must be born again. Paul told us *how* to be born again in Romans 10:9,10:

> **That if thou shalt confess with thy mouth the Lord Jesus, and shalt believe in thine heart that God hath raised him from the dead, thou shalt be saved.**
>
> **For with the *heart* man believeth unto righteousness; and with the mouth confession is made unto salvation.**

How can you be born again? Let's read between the lines. The first thing to understand about what Jesus said to Nicodemus is the times and the setting in which Jesus lived and ministered. When Nicodemus came to Him secretly by night, Jesus was just beginning His ministry. Apparently Nicodemus was one of those who believed because they saw the miracles that Jesus did. (John 2:23.) However, John wrote that Jesus did not commit Himself to them, because He *knew* what they really were like. (John 2:24.)

In other words, Jesus knew their belief was simply mental, of the soul, and not of the heart. They did not really accept Him as Messiah.

Nicodemus was a Pharisee, a member of the Sanhedrin (the highest ruling council of Judea at the time), a noted teacher of the law, and a prestigious member of Jewish society. He was of those who believed that salvation was earned by works, by obedience to the Law.

However, Jesus said to him, in essence, "You call yourself a teacher of the Law and you do not know that salvation is of the heart?" (John 3:10-12.)

Through the prophets, God had told them many times that "obedience was better than sacrifice" (1 Sam. 15:22), and that in a future time, He would give them new hearts. His law would be written on hearts, not on tablets of stone or on scrolls. (2 Cor. 3:2,3.)

Nicodemus was an educated man, but his education had not prepared him to understand what Jesus was saying. He was a man in authority, who had others coming to him for orders and instructions, yet he could not understand the simple truth Jesus was presenting to him.

You need to watch out for those folks who approach you with flowery words like Nicodemus did Jesus. In John 3:3, notice that Jesus totally ignored all of the good things the Jewish leader said, and answered what he should have asked.

A lot of people equate Nicodemus with a believer, but nothing in John 3 tells us that he made a positive response to what Jesus said.

Also, he was there with the Pharisees when the soldiers sent out to arrest Jesus returned saying they could not do it. They had never heard anyone speak like this Man, they said. (John 7:46.)

Nicodemus did speak up at that time to try and get Jesus a fair hearing, and the other Pharisees asked him, "What? Are you also from Galilee? Don't you know no prophet comes out of Galilee?" (John 7:50-53.)

But they did not know the scriptures very well, for Isaiah had prophesied exactly that: a "great light" was to come out of the land of Zebulun and Naphtali (Galilee). (Isa. 9:1,2.)

And the Bible says that every one of them then departed to his own house. So Nicodemus left with them and went home. However, after the crucifixion, he *was* one of the Pharisees who helped with the burial of Jesus (John 19:39), but that is still no sign he became a true believer in his heart.

Jesus had been through the wilderness experience and been perfected through trial and temptation when Nicodemus approached Him the first time. Already He had "whipped the devil's head" by using the Word of God as a sword against him. You cannot fight God's people with fists, feet, or other natural means. Paul wrote that the *weapons* of our warfare are not carnal (of natural material) but are **mighty through God to the pulling down of strong holds** (2 Cor. 10:4).

What is a *stronghold?* A stronghold is an unsanctified, fortified (walled-off) area in your mind that has made a place for a demon to attach himself. He has been there so long that deep down in your subconscious, he has built in an automatic ungodly reaction to something. When things occur that trigger that stronghold, your "string is pulled," and you find yourself doing things or making responses that you do not intend to make but cannot seem to stop making.

These can be things like we were talking about in chapter 7. If you feel dumb, you will act dumb. If you have bitterness, it becomes a stronghold, and the enemy uses it to cause your fruit to be bitter and instead of displaying the fruits of the Spirit (Gal. 5:22,23), you will defile others around you. (Heb. 12:15.)

Jesus said the ultimate *evidence* of salvation is the fruit you show. (Matt. 7:16.) In Matthew 13:18-23 in the Parable of the Sower, Jesus described four kinds of ground, a symbol for four kinds of heart and how each receives the Word of God. Only the fourth type involves salvation, and only the fourth bears fruit.

The seed in that parable is the message of the Gospel, which cannot take root and produce fruit in soil overgrown with weeds or in shallow soil. The Word-seed is taken in briefly by the mind but is soon choked out by the cares and weights of the world or because it does not reach the deep ground of the heart. We see some people get quickly "saved" and as quickly seem to backslide or fall away. Those are the ones in whom the seed never really took root to transform bad ground to good.

The seed that fell on the "wayside" had no effect at all. Those by the wayside are the ones who never even accept the Gospel in their minds. The evidence of salvation is not hearing the Word, reacting emotionally to the worship service, nor doing the works a Christian ought to be doing. The evidence is in the fruit.

You can confess with your mouth the Lord Jesus and *not* have a change of heart. You can confess Him aloud, yet go right out and continue sinning. That is not salvation. The evidence of salvation is a *changed life*. If your lifestyle has not changed since you were "converted," you better take another look at salvation.

Jesus said *many* would stand before Him in the Judgment — even those who preach, teach, and do signs and wonders — but He would have to say, "I not only don't know you, I *never* knew you. Depart from My presence." (Matt. 7:23.)

The Process of Sanctification

Of course, I do not mean that when you get saved, the old nature automatically dies. Not all good ground produces the same amount of fruit, according to Jesus. Some produced thirtyfold, some sixty, and some an hundredfold. (Mark 4:20.) But good ground always produces *some fruit*: love, joy, peace, patience, and the other fruits of the Spirit listed in Galatians 5:22,23.

Sanctification is the process of salvation of the soul that Paul called *"working* out your salvation day by day." (Phil. 2:12.) When he wrote that, he was not contradicting Jesus or saying that salvation is of works. The Bible says that salvation is a matter of God's mercy and grace and cannot be earned. (Eph. 2:8-10.)

The instantaneous change that occurs at conversion involves the spirits of people. The spirit being, who is the real you and will walk out of your body at death, is to be changed in the twinkling of an eye into a *new man*, one in the image of God and brought alive (connected to God) by the Holy Spirit. Paul wrote that the bodies of men and women who are children of God also will be "saved" (changed from corruptible to incorruptible) in "the twinkling of an eye." (1 Cor. 15:51-54.)

However, the soul — mind, will, and emotions — is a different matter. Because the right to choose that God gave every human being is involved, you must make choices day by day for the soul to be "saved" (a process the Church calls sanctification). You are not responsible for the inner man being of a fallen nature, because you inherited it from Adam and Eve; likewise, you inherited your body.

In other words, you made no choices for spirit and body to be the way they are, and nothing you can do could ever change them. So God sovereignly makes you a new person and will give you a new body at the resurrection. All you have to do is take a step of faith and *believe* on Jesus in your heart.

However, if you have been made a new person, there is no chance you will not appear changed in some ways to those around you. Usually, the change shows up as not liking the things of the world in which you used to be involved and, suddenly, loving the things of God.

From that point on, while God sees you wearing the "robe of righteousness" of Jesus (1 Cor. 1:30; 2 Cor. 5:21), the Holy Spirit is busy cleaning up your soul to match that robe. That is called "conforming to the image of Jesus." (Rom. 8:29.) You do that by choosing against things not like God in you and allowing the Holy Spirit to change those things.

There are several types of people who miss God:

1. Those who knowingly turn Him down,

2. Those who never hear of Him and do not seek Him through looking at His creation and becoming aware of His existence (Rom. 1),

3. Those who think they are not "good enough" (again, an emphasis on man's works instead of God's grace),

4. Those like King Agrippa, who are not yet ready to give up worldly things (Acts 26:28),

5. Those who think they are saved because they believe in their minds that there is a God, that Jesus was born and died on the cross for them, yet there has been no "heart change."

If you truly are converted, when you engage in the things of the old nature, you will feel convicted — not condemned. Religion condemns; the Holy Spirit convicts. Then you can repent, go through deliverance, get counseling, pray through, or do whatever is necessary to deal with the desire to do those things.

If you fall, you keep getting up. You change from day to day, because you are filled with the Holy Spirit. The old nature will drive you to do things that are comfortable to it, things you use to do and that your soul is accustomed to finding comfort in doing.

If you can go to church on Sunday, read your Bible, and even pray, yet feel it is okay to engage in drinking, fornicating, watching or reading ungodly things, and generally participating in the things of the world, then you need to take another look at salvation. You do not act like a changed, converted person.

Religion is not a relationship with God. It is a manmade system placed between man and God. The Pharisees were religious, and they had developed a system — Judaism — which they followed instead of God's Word. The system was man's interpretations and explanations of what God had said or meant. Jesus called that "traditions and doctrines of men." (Matt. 15:4-9.) And He called the scribes and Pharisees "hypocrites." (Matt. 23:13.)

They believed their group was so much more righteous than others that they separated themselves, not even allowing their clothes to touch those less religious. Today, denominationalism is Phariseeism, a man-made structure put between us and God. "Independent" churches that follow a certain "wave of God," a certain movement, or a certain man or woman, also can be Phariseeism.

Christian groups, ministries, or churches had better not ever get to the point of thinking they are the only ones with revelation, the only ones who can pray, or the only ones who have the right doctrine.

Thinking, "We're the only right ones, we're the only ones with the truth," will cause you to be susceptible to a spirit of heresy or to what the Pentecostals called "wildfire," supernatural happenings that are wild and outside of, or from another source than the Holy Spirit.

Conviction that leads to salvation is the revelation from the Holy Spirit that man, in his natural state, stinks in the nostrils of God and must be changed by God to a new creature, the member of a new race, born of the last Adam and the Second Man, Jesus.

Just as in chapter 7, the fruit shows what the tree is: If you call yourself an apple tree, but you are bearing rotten bananas, I have a problem with your salvation. Apples ought to produce apples. If you call yourself an apple tree, and your fruit is wormy, stunted, or has abnormalities, then you certainly have a problem, *but you are still an apple.* You need pruning, watering, fertilizing, and good plant food, and you will change your fruit from day to day. You will begin to conform your soul to the image of Jesus.

But if you are producing anything but apples, you need to be saved. You need to be transformed from one kind of tree to another. There are people walking the aisles of my church who are not a bit more regenerated than the man in the moon. If you cannot walk the Christian walk, at least some of the time, you have not been regenerated.

On the other hand, you cannot look at a man's good works and know whether or not he is born again. Only God knows the hearts of men. (Acts 1:24; 15:8.) Some of the largest "good and charitable works" in my city are not of God and are not blessed by Him.

You become a son or a daughter of God by adoption. (Rom. 8:15; Gal. 4:5.) If you are a true son or daughter, there will come a time of spiritual maturity when people do not have to say, "You sinned. You did wrong." You will know from the Holy Spirit. Your conscience will give a twinge, and you will say, "I've sinned against God. I must repent."

Isaiah 1:18,19 says:

> . . . Though your sins be as scarlet, they shall be as white as snow, though they be red like crimson, they shall be as wool.
>
> If ye be willing and obedient, ye shall eat of the good of the land.

God Saves Us for His Name's Sake

Blessings follow conversion. However, sometimes we tend to think God sent Jesus just for our benefit. We think God's work of cleansing us from sin is out of His great love for us — which it is, of course. However, there is more to it than that. First John 3:8 says that the purpose for which Jesus came was *to defeat the works of Satan.* Redeeming mankind from the penalty of sin and death was only part of the works of Satan.

Satan's works involve the state of all creation. The earth itself and all of the plants, animals, fish, and flying things were affected by the fall of Adam and Eve. The earth's governing, educational, cultural, entertainment, and all other systems are basically ungodly and Antichrist. They are classed among the works of Satan, which is why the devil could tempt Christ with the "kingdoms of this world" and why Jesus called the devil the "prince of this world. " (John 12:31.)

God provided a way to wash us "whiter than snow" for *His* own sake as well as to save mankind. Do you think He was going to let the devil win? God will not be defeated, nor will His purposes not be achieved. Throughout the history of man, God's purposes have steadily moved toward their ordained end. Satan wins some battles, but already has lost the war. His end is predetermined. (Rev. 20.)

In Ezekiel 36, God told Israel why He was willing to cleanse them and forgive their sins, and the same reason applies to us today.

> **But I had pity for mine holy name, which the house of Israel had profaned among the heathen, whither they went.**
>
> **Therefore say unto the house of Israel, Thus saith the Lord God; I do not do this for your sakes, 0 house of Israel, but for mine holy name's sake, which ye have profaned among the heathen, whither ye went.**
>
> **And I will sanctify my great name ... and the heathen shall know that I am the Lord, saith the Lord God, when I shall be sanctified in you before their eyes.**
>
> **Ezekiel 36:21-23**

In the New Testament, we find the Church is "the Israel of God" (Gal. 6:16.) I believe that today, God is saying to the Body of Christ:

"I am going to restore My people, the Church, but not because of you. I am going to restore it because My name is on it. You have profaned My name among the heathen, and for that reason — not for your sakes — I am going to restore you."

Today, God's name has been slandered. Folks want to jeer and joke about God, Jesus, and the Holy Spirit because those who have been professing the name of Deity have made God look bad. We are in the midst of the heathen, and we are not living the life Jesus told us to live in the Sermon on the Mount. (Matt. 5,6,7.)

God's people, individually and corporately, are so dysfunctional, according to His principles of conduct and order, that we have given God a bad name. But *change is coming*. That is why He warns His people of any generation not to set themselves with evildoers, unless they want to suffer the fate of evildoers. (Ps. 75:10, 101:8.)

In his epistle, Peter quoted the prophet Isaiah's saying that all mankind is like grass, here for a little while, then withering away, but the Word of God will last forever. (Isa. 40:6,7; 1 Pet. 1:24.) Anyone who thinks he always has time to get saved is a foolish person.

So revivals and restorations really are about clearing God's name. Salvation and sanctification are for the purpose of causing God's name to be strong and mighty. God wants to bring new life into His Church. He wants it to be *functional* in His way, not a valley of dry bones, such as Ezekiel saw, as recorded in chapter 37.

Ezekiel said the bones he saw were "very dry." (v. 2.) That means those people were dead. If you do not have the Word of God in you, you are dry ground. I have been invited to "dry" places and never been invited back, because the flood came in the Person of the Holy Spirit, and they could not receive it.

Incidentally, please do not send demons to "dry places," because that is where people are that do not have the Word. Those demons may find a place to live in dry places. Send them to "wet" places, where the Word of God is at such a floodtide there is no place for them. The Bible says to "give no place to the devil." (Eph. 4:27.)

But Ezekiel was told to "prophesy" over the bones. In his day, prophesying meant "preaching." What we call "prophesying" today was called "foreseeing" in Ezekiel's day. He was a *prophet* (a preacher) and a *seer* (what we call a prophet).

You cannot preach something to someone that God has not told you to preach to them. If you do, it is not true "preaching," but soulish, or fleshly, speaking forth things out of your own mind and knowledge. The life that is administered to people comes from "thus saith the Lord." All God needs is a "mouthpiece." That is what Ezekiel was, and that is what God's ministers of the five-fold offices are supposed to be today.

In verse 9, God said to Ezekiel to "prophesy" to the wind and breath came from the four winds to breathe upon the slain that they might live. So Ezekiel did what the Lord commanded him, and breath came into the bones, and they lived. They stood upon their feet, "an exceeding great army."

So we see that the army of the Lord is made up of those who have His life breathed into them, who are "wet" and not dry ground. God's army is made up of those who are full of His Word and whose spiritual ears are tuned to the voice of the Spirit. God's army will not be dysfunctional, but will function according to His will and purpose.

Do you want to be a functional member of the army of the Lord?

Do you want to be free of past bondages, bitter roots, and demonic strongholds?

Then find a church that believes in preaching the whole counsel of God, one that has a pastor who truly cares for the Body of Christ and is sincerely trying to equip the saints for the work of the ministry. Seek the guidance of the Holy Spirit on your own, and diligently study the Bible.

Teaching Tapes/Videos/Books
By William T. Jones, Jr.

The Dysfunctional Church Series I - $65.00

WJ	515	Dysfunctional Families..........No.	1
WJ	516	Contaminants of the Spirit.........No.	2
WJ	517	Spirit of Bondage.........No.	3
WJ	518	Denial.........No.	4
WJ	519	Fault Finding ....No.	5
WJ	520	Grudgeness ....No.	6
WJ	521	Bondage of Jealousy ....No.	7
WJ	522	Bitterness ....No.	8
WJ	523	Discouragement ....No.	9
WJ	524	Soul Ties ....No.	10
WJ	525	Addictive Behavior.........No.	11
WJ	526	Addictions ....No.	12
WJ	527	Depression..........No.	13
WJ	528	Discouragement ....No.	14
WJ	529	Spirit of Pride.........No.	15
WJ	530	Personality & Authority of a Champion ....No.	16

The Dysfunctional Church Series II - $20.00

WJ	531	The Purpose of the Church's Existence ....No.	1
WJ	532	Hidden Agenda in the Church. ....No.	2
WJ	533	The Church in Relationship to the Holy Spirit.........No.	3
WJ	534	The Tragedy of Being in the Wrong Church..No.	4

Single Series - $5.00

WJ	417	Healing the Dysfunctional Church ....No.	1
WJ	418	Abusing the Liberty of God.........No.	2
WJ	419	The Cost of the Circumcised Heart ....No.	3
WJ	420	Boys in the Hood.........No.	4
WJ	421	Boys to Men ....No.	5
WJ	422	Tragedy of Stumbling Over the Pulpit. ....No.	6

Fear Series - $20.00

WJ	423	Breaking the Fear That Has You Stuck ....No.	1
WJ	424	Fear & the Divided Heart ....No.	2
WJ	425	Fear & the Divided Heart ....No.	3
WJ	426	Plotting the Course for Continuous Victory ..No.	4

Restoration Series - $10.00

WJ 427 Restoration of a Black Man's Soul ....No. 1
WJ 428 Restoration of a Black Man's Soul ....No. 2

Discipleship Series - $10.00

WJ 429 True Discipleship ....No. 1
WJ 430 True Discipleship ....No. 2

Storms of Life Series - $10.00

WJ 431 When the Storms of Life Are Raging......................No 1
WJ 432 Sovereign Struggles:
         Godly Protection & Provision ....No. 2

The Anointing Series - $10.00

WJ 433 In Search of the Anointing ....No. 1
WJ 434 In Search of the Anointing ....No. 2

Video Series - $20.00

WJ 435 Sex, Sexuality and the Saints ....No. 1
WJ 436 God Is There...No. 2
WJ 437 Beauty for Ashes ....No. 3
WJ 438 Getting in the Birthing Position. ....No. 4

Books - $4.95

WJ 439 Vocabulary ....No. 1
WJ 440 Discerning False Prophets......................................No.
WJ 441 Discerning Between "Bondage" & "Captivity" ....No. 3
WJ 442 Healing the Believer's Jurisdictional Right & Privilege No. 4
WJ 443 Restoration of a Black Man's Soul ....No. 5
WJ 444 Victory Through Jesus...No. 6

Teaching Tapes
By Willie Izetta Jones

Single Tape - $5.00

WWJ 450 What God Hates...No. 1
WWJ 451 You Can't Get To Know God in Your Flesh...........No. 2
WWJ 452 The Time Is Now ....No. 3
WWJ 453 Stop Living Your Life Out of Your Fears................No. 4
WWJ 454 Shame..No. 5

Send Order To:
(Please Print Clearly)

Name: _____

Address: _____

City: _____ State: _____

Zip: _____

Tape No.	Quantity	Amount
Shipping & Handling		
TOTAL		

Mail To: Greater Mount Zion Christian Fellowship
2212 Chambers Road • St. Louis, MO 63136